Golf's Most
Wanted

Also by Floyd Conner

Golf's Most
Wanted

The Top 10 Book of the
Great Game's Outrageous Duffers,
Deadly Divots, and Other Oddities

Floyd Conner

Brassey's, Inc.

WASHINGTON, D.C.

Library of Congress Cataloging-in-Publication Data

Conner, Floyd, 1951-
    Golf's most wanted : the top ten book of the great games's outrageous duffers, deadly divots, and other oddities / Floyd Conner.
        p.   cm.
    ISBN 1-57488-360-7 (alk. paper)
    1. Golf--Miscellanea. I. Title: Top ten book of the great game's outrageous duffers, deadly divots, and other oddities. II. Title.

GV967 .C595 2001
796.352—dc21

                                                    2001025100

Printed in Canada

Brassey's
22841 Quicksilver Drive
Dulles, Virginia 20166

Designed by Pen & Palette Unlimited

Photographs courtesy of USGA

First Edition

10 9 8 7 6 5 4 3 2 1

Contents

List of Photographs

Introduction

Golf originated in Europe 500 years ago. The game made its debut in the United States in 1888 when John Reid converted a cow pasture in Yonkers, New York, into the nation's first golf course. In the last one hundred years, golf has become one of the world's most popular recreational activities. With the emergence of superstar Tiger Woods, the popularity of golf as a spectator sport is at an all-time high. The PGA, LPGA, and Senior tours have legions of devoted fans.

Golf's Most Wanted pays tribute to the sport's most outrageous characters. The book contains top-ten lists of the worst players, most unplayable lies, and craziest shots in golf history. The lists feature the unlikeliest heroes, most preposterous penalties, wildest spectators, bad-tempered players, fantastic finishes, and the most unusual things ever to take place on a golf course.

In the game of golf, anything can happen. Margaret Abbott won the gold medal in women's golf at the 1900 Paris Olympics without even knowing that she was competing in the Olympic games. Monica Hannah won a tournament despite being nine months pregnant. Harry Dearth played a round of golf while dressed in a suit of armor. Alex Campbell lost the 1907 U.S. Open Championship because the experimental air-filled pneumatic golf ball he was using deflated. Bobby Jones, the only golfer to win the Grand Slam, retained his amateur status throughout his career and never earned a cent for playing the game.

An errant golf shot can end up in some unlikely places. Sam Snead once hit a ball into a men's bathroom. Hale Irwin hit a ball into a woman's brassiere. Harry Bradshaw lost the 1949 British Open because one of his shots landed in a broken beer bottle. Raymond Floyd hit a shot into his own golf bag. One of Oscar Grimes's shots landed in a cash register.

Golf has its share of inspiring stories. Babe Zaharias, diagnosed with cancer in 1953, came back a year later to win the U.S. Women's Open Championship by 12 strokes. Severely wounded during World War I, Tommy Armour won three majors after the war. Armless golfer Jim Taylor made eight holes-in-one. Ninety-nine-year-old Otto Bucher proved you are never too old to play golf by scoring a hole-in-one.

Golf can be a frustrating game. Chevalier von Cittern set a record for ineptitude by taking 316 strokes to complete an 18-hole round. Angelo Spagnola shot a round of 257 to earn the title of being the worst avid golfer in America. A. J. Lewis once made 156 putts on one hole and still did not sink one. At the 1979 Dryden Invitational, T. J. Moore hit 20 consecutive shots into the water. Edith Bolling Wilson, wife of President Woodrow Wilson, once took 17 shots to hit a ball out of a mud puddle.

The rules of golf can be cruel. J. C. Snead was penalized for putting with his hat. Andy Bean lost the Canadian Open by making a putt with the wrong end of his club. Jack Fleck was penalized eight strokes for taking practice swings. Tommy Bolt was fined for breaking wind in a tournament. Porky Oliver was disqualified from the 1940 U.S. Open Championship for teeing off too early.

Golf has been known to drive players crazy. Professional golfer Clayton Heafner dismantled his car following a disastrous round. Lefty Stackhouse punched himself out after hitting a poor shot. Ky Laffoon tried to kill his putter after missing a short putt. Ivan Gantz threw himself face first into a bunker in the midst of a temper tantrum. President Gerald Ford once was given a trophy for the longest putter throw.

Golfers occasionally make friendly wagers. Payne Stewart lost his knickers in a bet with three women professional golfers. Millionaire John F. Kennedy bet 10 cents a hole. Billionaire Howard Hughes employed a nude starlet to distract opponents in order to win a bet. In 1930, golfer Bobby Cruickshank won more than $100,000 betting that Bobby Jones would win the Grand Slam.

A round of golf can resemble an African safari. Richard Blackman was chased off a golf course by a lion. Jimmy Stewart, the golfer, not the actor, was attacked by a cobra that mistook his golf ball for an egg. Sam Snead suffered a hand injury when he was bitten by an ostrich. During an exhibition in South Africa, Gary Player and Jack Nicklaus ran for their lives after disturbing a hive of killer bees.

At times golf can be hazardous to your health. Bayly MacArthur barely escaped with his life after slipping into a quicksand trap. Gangster Al Capone shot himself in the foot while playing. George Bush once beaned his vice president, Dan Quayle, with an errant shot. Another president, John F.

Kennedy, flipped his golf cart into a lake while trying to cross a narrow bridge.

This book introduces you to nearly 700 of golf's most wanted players. Their offenses range from inept play to outrageous behavior. Be on the lookout for these individuals.

The First Hole

The 1922 U.S. Open, held at the Skokie Country Club in Illinois, was the first tournament in which an admission fee was charged for spectators. The following list features some of golf's most notable firsts.

1. *KOLF*

The name golf is derived from the Dutch word, *kolf,* which means club. An early version of the game called *spel meten kolven* was played in the Netherlands as early as the thirteenth century. Dutch traders introduced the game to Scotland in the fifteenth century. Golf quickly became a popular diversion in Scotland. In 1457, King James II temporarily banned the game because Scottish men were spending so much time playing golf that their archery skills suffered.

2. ALVIN ROBERTSON

The first golf professional was Alvin Robertson. He was a golf pro at the Royal and Ancient Golf Club of St. Andrews, Scotland, in the 1840s.

3. JOHN REID

Golf was played in Charleston, South Carolina, as early as 1743. The first golf club in the United States was the St. Andrews Club of Yonkers, New York. It was founded in 1888 by a Scotsman named John Reid. The original course consisted of only six holes. In 1897, the first 18-hole course in America opened in Mt. Hope, New York.

4. WILLIE PARK

The inaugural British Open was held on a 12-hole golf course in 1860. All three rounds were played in a single day. The winner, Willie Park, was awarded a red Moroccan leather belt for his victory. The first twelve British Opens were played at Prestwick, Scotland.

5. HORACE RAWLINS

In 1895, he first U.S. Open Championship was played at the Newport Golf Club in Rhode Island. Nineteen-year-old Horace Rawlins won the tournament. An amateur tournament was also held which was won by Charles Macdonald.

6. GEORGE GRANT

In 1899, an African American dentist named George Grant patented the first golf tee. Up until that time golfers teed their balls on a mound made of a mixture of sand and water. Grant never marketed his invention. Twenty-two years later, another dentist, William Lowell introduced the Reddy Tee. At first, golfers refused to use the tees, even when Lowell handed them out free of charge. Only when he paid champion golfer Walter Hagen $1,500 to use them did the tees gain wide acceptance.

7. **DAVID HUNTER**

David Hunter shot the first sub-70 round in the history of the U.S. Open Championship. In 1909, he shot 68 in the morning round, then ballooned to an 84 in the afternoon. Hunter finished 23 shots behind the winner, George Sargent.

8. **BILLY BURKE**

Former ironworker Billy Burke was the first golfer to win the U.S. Open Championship using steel-shafted clubs. Burke won the 1931 Open, played at the Inverness Club in Toledo, Ohio. All the previous winners had played with wooden-shafted clubs.

9. **GENE SARAZEN**

Like most golfers of the 1920s, Gene Sarazen had difficulty with his bunker shots. The thin-bladed niblicks used at that time were not suited for sand play. Sarazen soldered lead onto the back of his niblick, which permitted him to explode his shots and land them softly on the green. When Sarazen played in the 1932 British Open, he kept his new sand wedge a secret, afraid that the new club might be declared illegal. Sarazen's wedge helped him win the Open with a record 72-hole score of 283.

10. **JERRY PATE**

Jerry Pate holds the distinction of being the first golfer to jump into a water hazard following a tournament victory. Pate promised he would "bathe in victory" if he won the 1981 Danny Thomas Memphis Classic, at the Colonial Country Club. He kept his promise and dove fully clothed into a lake near the 18th green.

Tiger Tales

No golfer has accomplished so much at such an early age as Tiger Woods. He has won three consecutive United States Amateur Championships, a feat not even the great Bobby Jones accomplished. At age 24, he was the youngest player ever to complete the Grand Slam, winning the Masters in 1997, the PGA Championship in 1999 and 2000, and the British and United States Opens in 2000. Groomed to be a champion golfer by his father, Tiger picked up his first golf club when he was only 9 months old.

1. *THE MIKE DOUGLAS SHOW*

At age 2, Tiger appeared on *The Mike Douglas Show*. Guest Bob Hope, an avid golfer, challenged the youngster to a putting contest. After missing three putts, Tiger complained that the putting green was not level.

2. BREAKING 50 FOR NINE HOLES

Tiger was only 3 years old when he broke 50 for nine holes for the first time. He shot 48 while playing from the red tees at the Destroyer Golf Course. Woods carried only three clubs in his bag.

3. BREAKING 60 ON PAR-3 COURSE

At age 4, Tiger Woods shot 59 on the par-54 Heartwell Golf Park course in Long Beach, California. All the holes on the course were par 3s.

4. THAT'S INCREDIBLE

Woods's golfing skills were so remarkable that at age 5 he was featured in a segment on the television program *That's Incredible.* Tiger sat in host Fran Tarkenton's lap and hit whiffle balls into the studio audience.

5. BREAKING 100 FOR 18 HOLES

Tiger Woods was given his first full set of golf clubs when he was 5 years old. That year, he shot in the 90s for the first time on a regulation-length 18-hole golf course.

6. FIRST HOLE-IN-ONE

Woods was 6 years old when he scored his first hole-in-one. He was already good enough to play competitively with professional golfers. In a match with pro Stewart Reed, Tiger led for nine holes before the more experienced player rallied for a narrow victory. Tiger was so upset that he left the course in tears. He began listening to subliminal tape-recorded messages to increase his self-control.

7. EXHIBITION WITH SAM SNEAD

In 1982, 6-year-old Tiger Woods played a two-hole exhibition with the legendary Sam Snead. Woods bogeyed both holes while Snead made two pars. After the round, Snead offered his autograph to the young Tiger. Woods responded by offering to sign an autograph for Snead.

8. **WINNING WORLD JUNIOR TOURNAMENT**

Woods was 8 years old when he broke 80 for the first time. He also won the Junior World Ten-and-Under golf tournament against many older players.

9. **BREAKING 70 THE FIRST TIME**

Breaking 70 is a milestone for any golfer. Tiger Woods was only 12 years old when he shot in the 60s for the first time.

10. **INSURANCE YOUTH GOLF CLASSIC**

When he was 13 years old, Tiger played a round with John Daly in the Insurance Youth Golf Classic at the Texarkana Country Club in Arkansas. At the turn, Woods was 3 under par, two shots better than Daly, who was several years his elder. Daly, fearful of losing to a 13-year-old, birdied four holes to pull out the match. Woods finished second in the tournament, which featured 20 professional and 60 junior golfers.

Golf Prodigies

Tiger Woods was only 21 years old when he won his first Masters in 1997. All the following golfers displayed remarkable golfing skills before age 21.

1. SCOTT STATLER

Scott Statler was only 4 years old when he accomplished something most golfers only dream of. On July 30, 1962, he scored a hole-in-one on the seventh hole at the Statler's Par 3 Golf Course in Greensburg, Pennsylvania.

2. BRITTNY ANDREAS

The youngest girl to record a hole-in-one was 6-year-old Brittny Andreas. She aced the second hole at the Jimmy Clay Golf Course in Austin, Texas, in 1991.

3. BEVERLY KLASS

Incredibly, Beverly Klass was only 10 years old when she began playing on the LPGA Tour. She played in three events in 1967. Her career was interrupted when the LPGA passed a rule that a golfer must be age 18 to compete on the tour.

Nine years later, Klass returned to the LPGA Tour, and in 1978, she set a record for the fewest putts in a round (19) at the 1978 Women's International, in Hilton Head, South Carolina.

4. **MARTHA BURKARD**

Twelve-year-old Martha Burkard won the 2000 San Francisco Women's Golf Championship with a 2 up victory over 22-year-old Edna Anderson in a match played at the Harding Park Golf Course. Burkard was five years younger than the previous youngest winner in this 73-year-old event.

5. **THUASHNI SELVARATNAM**

In 1989, Thuashni Selvaratnam became the youngest golfer to win a national championship. The 12-year-old won the Sri Lanka Amateur Golf Championship played at Nuvvara Eliya Golf Course.

6. **LAURA BAUGH**

At age 16, Laura Baugh became the youngest golfer to win the U.S. Women's Amateur Championship, a feat she accomplished in 1971. In 20 years on the LPGA Tour, Baugh never won a tournament, but she was one of its most popular players. In 1972, she was voted The Most Beautiful Golfer.

7. **TOM MORRIS, JR.**

Tom Morris, Jr. was 17 years old when he won the 1868 British Open, played at Prestwick, Scotland, making him the youngest golfer ever to win the event. He won three more championships, becoming the only golfer to win four consecutive British Opens. His father, Tom Morris, Sr., was 46

Laura Baugh

Known more for her good looks than for her playing abilities, the only title Laura Baugh won in 20 years on the LPGA Tour was as the 1972 Most Beautiful Golfer.

when he won the 1867 British Open, making him the oldest
golfer to win the tournament.

8. MARLENE HAGGE

Marlene Hagge became the youngest woman to be victorious in an LPGA tournament when at age 18 she won the
1952 Sarasota Open in Florida. It was the first of 25 LPGA
tournament victories for Hagge.

9. JOHNNY MCDERMOTT

Nineteen-year-old Johnny McDermott won the 1911 U.S.
Open Championship, played at the Chicago Golf Club. The
next year, he proved his victory was no fluke by repeating
as Open champion at the Country Club of Buffalo. He
became the first golfer to break par in the U.S. Open, finishing the tournament with a 2-under-par 294.

   McDermott's brilliant career was curtailed by a series of
tragedies. Returning from the British Open on the ocean liner
Kaiser Wilhelm II, the ship collided with another vessel, *The
Incemore*. McDermott's ship sank, but he was rescued. His
near brush with death, coupled with losses in the stock mar-
ket, had disastrous effects on his mental health. By age 23,
McDermott's competitive golfing career was over.

10. GENE SARAZEN

Gene Sarazen was only 20 years old when he won the 1922
U.S. Open Championship, played at The Skokie Country Club
near Chicago. He defeated Bobby Jones and 43-year-old
John Black by one shot. A month later, Sarazen won the PGA
Championship, played at the Oakmont Country Club in
Pennsylvania.

You Are never Too Old

O ne of the great things about golf is that it is a game you can play at an advanced age. Sandy Herd was 58 years old when he won the 1926 News of the World Match Play Championship. Sixty-eight-year-old Harriet O'Brien Lee felt chipper enough to hole five chip shots during a round at the Meadows Golf Club in Grayeagle, California. Tom Morris, Sr. won the 1867 British Open when he was 46 years old and played in the tournament until he was 75.

1. ARTHUR THOMPSON

In 1973, Arthur Thompson shot 103 at the Uplands Golf Course in British Columbia, Canada. What made the round remarkable was that Thompson was 103 years old at the time, making him the oldest golfer ever to shoot his age.

2. OTTO BUCHER

The oldest golfer to score a hole-in-one was 99-year-old Otto Bucher. On January 13, 1985, the Swiss golfer holed his tee shot on the 130-yard 12th hole of the La Manga Golf Course in Spain.

3. ERNA ROSS

Erna Ross was the oldest woman golfer to make a hole-in-one. She was 95 when she aced the 112-yard 17th hole at the Everglades Golf Club in Palm Beach, Florida, on May 25, 1986.

4. GEORGE SMITH

It is a rarity when a golfer shoots his age. George Smith is the only golfer to shoot 15 strokes less than his age. The 90-year-old golfer shot 75 at the Cypress Lake Golf Club in Fort Myers, Florida, in 1988.

5. CHARLIE LAW

Another golfer who shot a score less than his age was Charlie Law. On May 20, 1984, the 84-year-old Law shot 75 at the Hayston Golf Course in Scotland.

6. JERRY BARBER

Forty-five-year-old Jerry Barber won the 1961 PGA Championship, played at the Olympia Fields Country Club in Illinois. Barber competed on the Senior Tour well into his seventies. In 1992, Barber was 75 when he led the Senior Tour in driving accuracy. In fact, his 82.7 percent accuracy rate was higher than the leader on the PGA tour.

7. GENE SARAZEN

In 1973, Gene Sarazen became the oldest player to score a hole-in-one in the history of the British Open. The 71-year-old golfing legend aced the famed Postage Stamp Hole at the Royal Troon Golf Course in Scotland. More than 40 years earlier, Sarazen had won the 1932 British Open.

8. **SAM SnEAD**

Ageless Sam Snead became the oldest golfer ever to win a PGA event when he captured the 1965 Greater Greensboro Open at age 52. Four years later, Snead lost a playoff to Tommy Aaron at the Canadian Open. He also finished second at age 61 in the 1974 Los Angeles Open. Later that year, Snead finished third in the 1974 PGA Championship, behind Lee Trevino and Jack Nicklaus. The 67-year-old Snead shot rounds of 67 and 66 in the 1979 Quad Cities Open.

9. **MIKE FETCHICK**

Mike Fetchick won the 1985 Hilton Head Seniors International in South Carolina on his sixty-third birthday. Fetchick entered the record book as the oldest golfer to win a tournament on the Senior Tour.

10. **ROBERT KLInGAMAn**

On August 31, 1971, Robert Klingaman became the youngest golfer to shoot his age. The 58-year-old Klingaman fired a round of 58 at the Caledon Golf Club in Pennsylvania.

Senior Stardom

The Senior Tour gave second chances to many golfers who did not excel on the regular PGA Tour. Walter Morgan never played on the PGA Tour but won the 1995 GTE Northwest Classic and two more tournaments on the Senior Tour in 1996. Dana Quigley, another multiple winner on the Senior Tour, was also winless on the PGA Tour. For each of these golfers, life began at 50.

1. JIM DENT

Despite being one of the longest hitters in golf, Jim Dent was winless in 19 years on the PGA Tour. He blossomed on the Senior Tour, winning 11 events and more than $5 million in prize money. Dent won four tournaments in 1990 alone.

2. ORVILLE MOODY

Orville Moody's only victory on the PGA Tour was the 1969 U.S. Open Championship. On the Senior Tour, Moody switched to a long putter to cure his putting woes. Between 1984 and 1992, Moody won 11 tournaments on the Senior Tour, most notably the 1989 U.S. Senior Open Championship.

3. **BRUCE FLEISHER**

Bruce Fleisher played in more than 400 events on the PGA Tour. His only victory came in the 1991 New England Classic. By contrast, Fleisher won 10 tournaments during his first 18 months on the Senior Tour and earned Player of the Year honors as a rookie.

4. **LARRY LAORETTI**

Larry Laoretti never played on the PGA Tour. When Laoretti entered the 1992 U.S. Senior Open Championship, the 53-year-old had never won a professional tournament. He shocked everyone by posting a four-stroke victory over Jim Colbert in the Open, played at the Saucon Valley Country Club in Bethlehem, Pennsylvania.

5. **GARY MCCORD**

Best known for his wry commentary as a golf announcer, Gary McCord never won a tournament on the PGA Tour. In 1999, McCord finally broke through with two victories on the Senior Tour.

6. **JIM ALBUS**

A club pro in Long Island, New York, Jim Albus earned only $3,750 in his career on the PGA Tour. In 1991, he won the Senior Players Championship by three strokes.

7. **BOB E. SMITH**

Bob E. Smith set a dubious record by playing on the PGA Tour for a quarter century without a win. The closest he came to victory were second place finishes at the 1973 B.C.

Open and 1975 Byron Nelson Classic. On the Senior Tour, he notched his first victory at the 1993 Yanase Cup in Japan.

8. **ROCKY THOMPSON**

Rocky Thompson was nicknamed "King Rabbit" on the PGA Tour because of the many times he had to qualify to get into tournaments. Never a winner on the PGA Tour, Thompson won both the Digital Seniors Classic and the MONY Syracuse Senior Classic in 1991.

9. **WALTER ZEMBRISKI**

A former construction worker, Walter Zembriski did not play on the PGA Tour. Zembriski was a two-time winner on the Senior Tour in 1988 and won the GTE West Classic in 1989.

10. **JIMMY POWELL**

In 1980, 45-year-old Jimmy Powell became the oldest golfer to graduate from the PGA Qualifying School. He earned only $27,796 on the tour. He was 55 when he won his first tournament on the Senior Tour, the 1990 Southwestern Bell Classic. Two years later, Powell won the 1992 Aetna Challenge.

Good Sports

Golfers often excel in other sports. Bunky Henry, who won the 1969 National Airlines Open on the PGA Tour, was a place kicker on the Georgia Tech football team. Joan Joyce, an outstanding pitcher in women's softball, set an LPGA record when she needed only 17 putts in a round of the 1982 Ladies Michelob Open. Baseball catcher Johnny Bench shot a round of 65 at the 1994 Hall of Fame Classic and has played in tournaments on the Senior Tour.

1. **BABE ZAHARIAS**

Babe Didrikson Zaharias is frequently called the greatest all-around female athlete. At the 1932 Summer Olympics, she won two gold medals. During her track-and-field career, she held world records in the javelin throw, long jump, high jump, and 80-meter hurdles. A Hall of Fame golfer, she won 31 tournaments on the LPGA Tour, including U.S. Open Championship titles in 1948, 1950, and 1954.

2. **HALE IRWIN**

Hale Irwin was a two-time All Big Eight Conference defensive back at the University of Colorado. A three-time U.S. Open

Championship winner, Irwin has been a superstar on both the PGA and Senior tours.

3. JOHN BRODIE

John Brodie played quarterback for the San Francisco 49ers from 1957 to 1973. He led the National Football League in passing in 1970. In 1991, Brodie won the Security Pacific Senior Classic played at the Rancho Park Golf Course in Los Angeles.

4. ALTHEA GIBSON

The first African American to win a major tennis tournament, Althea Gibson was the Wimbledon and U.S. Open champion in both 1957 and 1958. Following her tennis career, Gibson played on the LPGA Tour from 1964 to 1969.

5. CHARLOTTE DOD

Charlotte Dod was only 15 years old when she won her first Wimbledon Championship. During her career, Dod won five Wimbledon tennis titles. Also an outstanding golfer, she won the Ladies' British Open in 1904.

6. ELLSWORTH VINES

Tennis great Ellsworth Vines won the U.S. Open and Wimbledon in 1932. He won the first professional golf tournament he entered, the 1945 Southern California Open.

7. SAMMY BYRD

Outfielder Sammy Byrd played major-league baseball from 1929 to 1936. He was nicknamed "Babe Ruth's Legs" because he frequently was a pinch-runner for Ruth late in his career. A scratch golfer, Byrd became a professional after

Althea Gibson

One of the twentieth century's most talented athletes, Gibson
pursued successful careers in both tennis and golf.

retiring from baseball. He won several tournaments, including the 1942 Greensboro Open and the 1943 New Orleans Open. Byrd reached the final match of the 1945 PGA Championship, losing to Sam Snead 4 and 3.

8. ROBERT GARDNER

Nineteen-year-old Robert Gardner won the 1909 U.S. Amateur Championship, played at the Chicago Golf Club. On June 1, 1912, he became the first person to pole vault higher than 13 feet. Three years later, Gardner won a second U.S. Amateur title.

9. RICK RHODEN

Rick Rhoden was a top starting pitcher for the Los Angeles Dodgers, Pittsburgh Pirates, and New York Yankees. He won 16 games with the Dodgers in 1977 and again with the Yankees in 1987. In recent years, Rhoden has dominated the Celebrity Players Tour. His victory in the 2000 Atlantic City Kids Golf Classic was his fifteenth on the tour and pushed his earnings over $1 million.

10. BOBBY KNIGHT

Bobby Knight coached Indiana University to three NCAA basketball championships. During a golf round in 1982 at the Indiana University Golf Course in Bloomington, his temper got the best of him. After he missed a short putt on the fifth hole, Knight threw his putter in the air in disgust. The putter got stuck high in a maple tree. Early the next morning, Knight climbed the tree in an attempt to retrieve his putter. Unable to reach the club, he remained in the tree for an hour, to avoid being seen by other golfers.

Celebrity Golfers

Golf has been a favorite recreational sport of entertainers and politicians. Bing Crosby and Bob Hope were low handicap golfers who hosted their own tournaments. Although less talented on the links, Groucho Marx and Jack Lemmon were nonetheless avid golfers.

1. BING CROSBY

Academy Award–winning actor Bing Crosby was one of Hollywood's most avid golfers. A player with a 2 handicap, Crosby was one of only four golfers to score a hole-in-one on the 16th hole of Cypress Point, California, considered by many to be the toughest par 3 in the world. From 1937 until his death, Crosby hosted his own pro-am tournament. For most of its existence, The Crosby was played at Pebble Beach Golf Course in California. Crosby died following a round of golf in Spain in 1977. His son, Nathaniel, was the 1981 U.S. Amateur champion.

2. BOB HOPE

Jimmy Demaret once said of Bob Hope, "He's got a great short game. Unfortunately, it's off the tee." In fact, Hope was

Bing Crosby

Bing loved golf almost as much as he loved show business. He hosted his own Pro-Am tournament for forty years.

a 4-handicap player in his prime. In 1949, he shot rounds of 74 and 73 to defeat his Road pictures' costar Bing Crosby by two shots at the National Celebrities Tournament in Washington, D.C. Since 1965, the Bob Hope Classic has been a stop on the PGA Tour.

3. BARRY FITZGERALD

In 1944, Barry Fitzgerald won an Academy Award for best supporting actor for his performance as a priest in the film *Going My Way.* During World War II, the Oscars were made of plaster because metal was being rationed. While Fitzgerald was practicing his golf swing at home, he accidentally struck and decapitated his Oscar. Fortunately, the Motion Picture Academy replaced the statuette.

4. GROUCHO MARX

Comedian Groucho Marx made a hole-in-one at the Brae Burn Country Club near Boston. The *Boston Globe* featured a photograph of Groucho next to golfing greats Bobby Jones and Walter Hagen. The caption read, "Groucho Joins the Immortals." The next day, Groucho agreed to replay the hole for the benefit of photographers. This time he was not so lucky. Unnerved by the onlookers, Groucho shot a 22 on the hole. The next day, the *Globe* carried the story with the headline "Groucho Leaves the Immortals."

Years later, Groucho hit his first five tee shots into the water on the treacherous 16th hole at Cypress Point in California. He threw his clubs into the ocean and vowed never to play again.

5. **DAN QUAYLE**

Dan Quayle, former vice president to George Bush, has the reputation of being one of the best golfers among politicians. At age 17, Quayle made his first hole-in-one. A year later he shot 68. Blessed with a beautiful swing, Quayle won many trophies as a teenager. He served as captain on his golf team at DePauw University. Quayle twice won his club championship in Fort Wayne, Indiana. During a pro-am at the Kemper Open, Quayle defeated his professional partner Joey Sindelar by four shots.

6. **HOWARD HUGHES**

Billionaire Howard Hughes was not always reclusive. As a young man, he was a scratch golfer. A frequent golfing companion was actress Katharine Hepburn. In 1938, he was scheduled to play a 1:00 P.M. match with Hepburn at the Bel-Air Country Club. At tee time, Hughes was nowhere to be found. Suddenly, Hughes's plane appeared and landed on the fairway. He emerged from the plane with his golf clubs and began play as if nothing unusual had happened. Fined $2,000 by the club, Hughes wrote a check and continued his round.

A serious golfer, Hughes asked Riviera Club pro Willie Hunter if he thought Hughes was good enough to win the U.S. Amateur Championship. When told he was not, Hughes quit the game.

7. **FRED ASTAIRE**

Fred Astaire performed one of the most amazing golf scenes on film in the 1938 movie *Carefree.* At a golf course in Pasadena, California, Astaire tap-danced while driving a dozen golf balls. Remarkably, all 12 balls landed on the green within 10 feet of one another.

8. **JACK LEMMON**

Actor Jack Lemmon would probably give one of his Oscars to play on the final day of the Pebble Beach Pro-Am. For more than 25 years, he played in the Pro-Am but was never able to qualify for the final round on Sunday. An exchange with a caddie sums up Lemmon's futility. After Lemmon asked the caddie which way a putt would break, the caddie answered, "Who cares?"

9. **BILL MURRAY**

Comedian Bill Murray was memorable as the exasperated greenskeeper battling a gopher in *Caddyshack*. A talented golfer, Murray is a frequent participant in pro-ams. Known for his comic antics on the course, Murray once tossed a woman spectator into a sand trap.

10. **W. C. FIELDS**

W. C. Fields enjoyed playing golf so much that he bought a house adjacent to a golf course. Fields despised the geese that landed in his yard. He could be seen chasing them with a niblick and yelling, "Either poop green or get off my lawn!"

Celebrity Golf Tournaments

Bing Crosby and Bob Hope are not the only entertainers who have had their own golf tournaments.

1. ANDY WILLIAMS

Singer Andy Williams has had 27 Top 40 hits and hosted television variety shows on all three major networks. From 1968 to 1988, Williams also hosted the Andy Williams Open in San Diego. Winners of the event included Jack Nicklaus, Tom Watson, and Johnny Miller.

2. DANNY THOMAS

Entertainer Danny Thomas is best remembered for starring in the popular sitcom *Make Room for Daddy,* which aired from 1953 to 1964. Thomas hosted the Memphis St. Jude Classic from 1970 to 1984. The tournament was won by such outstanding golfers as Lee Trevino, Gary Player, and Raymond Floyd.

3. DINAH SHORE

Television personality and singer Dinah Shore starred in her own variety show from 1951 to 1962. In 1972, the Nabisco

Dinah Shore Tournament was added to the LPGA Tour and in 1983, the event was recognized as a major tournament. Mickey Wright, Kathy Whitworth, and Nancy Lopez are among the winners of the Dinah Shore Tournament.

4. SAMMY DAVIS, JR.

Sammy Davis, Jr. was known as the world's greatest entertainer because of his multiple talents. From 1973 to 1988, Davis had his own PGA tournament, the Sammy Davis Greater Hartford Open. Winners of the tournament included Billy Casper, Curtis Strange, and Paul Azinger.

5. GLEN CAMPBELL

Glen Campbell had a string of Top 10 hits, most notably "Wichita Lineman," "Rhinestone Cowboy," and "Southern Nights." An avid golfer, he hosted the Glen Campbell Los Angeles Open from 1971 to 1983. Hale Irwin, Tom Watson, and Johnny Miller all were tournament winners.

6. JACKIE GLEASON

Jackie Gleason portrayed frustrated bus driver Ralph Kramden in the classic sitcom *The Honeymooners*. From 1972 to 1980, the Jackie Gleason Inverrary Classic in Florida was an event on the PGA Tour. Winners included Lee Trevino, Jack Nicklaus, and Johnny Miller.

7. JOE GARAGIOLA

Joe Garagiola was a catcher in the major leagues from 1946 to 1954 and a noted baseball announcer and television personality. Garagiola hosted the Tucson Open from 1977 to 1983.

8. **DEAN MARTIN**

Dean Martin was a star of film, television, radio, and music. Martin also hosted the Tucson Open from 1973 to 1975. Johnny Miller won the tournament in 1974 and 1975.

9. **ED MCMAHON**

For thirty years, Ed McMahon was Johnny Carson's sidekick on *The Tonight Show.* McMahon lent his name to the Quad City Open from 1975 to 1979.

10. **JAMIE FARR**

Jamie Farr played the cross-dressing Corporal Max Klinger in the television series *M*A*S*H.* In 1984, the Jamie Farr Toledo Classic became an LPGA tournament.

White House Golfers

Jimmy Demaret suggested that every presidential candidate should be required to play a round of golf to determine how well he could handle adversity. More than a dozen American presidents have been golfers since William McKinley first picked up a golf club in the late 1890s. Calvin Coolidge once took 11 shots to reach the green of a 130-yard hole. It was said that the penurious president did not hit balls very far because he was fearful of losing one. Before Franklin Roosevelt contracted polio at age 39, he was an excellent golfer known for his long drives. Roosevelt once won his club championship. He learned to play the game on a six-hole course his father had built on the family estate at Hyde Park, New York. Ronald Reagan practiced his putting in the Oval Office and aboard *Air Force One*. When asked what his handicap was, Reagan quipped, "Congress."

1. DWIGHT EISENHOWER

Although Dwight Eisenhower did not take up the game until he was 37 years old, he made up for lost time in his later years. During his presidency, which spanned from 1953 to 1961, Eisenhower played more than 800 rounds of golf. He had a putting green, complete with a sand trap, built on the White House lawn so that he could practice any time. A good player, Eisenhower once shot 79 at Augusta National, the course where The Masters is played. He actually outdrove Byron Nelson with a 260-yard smash. Eisenhower suggested that a loblolly pine on the 17th hole at Augusta be cut down because his shots frequently hit it. The tree remained and was known thereafter as the Eisenhower Tree.

While playing the Eldorado Golf Course in Palm Springs, Eisenhower hit into a grove of grapefruit trees and had a difficult time finding his ball among the fruit. When he returned to the White House, he threatened to fire anyone who served him grapefruit.

In 1968, a year before his death, the 77-year-old Eisenhower used a 9-iron to score a hole-in-one on the 13th hole at the Seven Lakes Country Club in Palm Springs. The man who had been the allied commander in Europe during World War II and president of the United States called his hole-in-one "the thrill of a lifetime."

2. WILLIAM HOWARD TAFT

Three hundred–pound William Howard Taft, president from 1909 to 1913, helped popularize the game of golf in America. Carrying only seven or eight clubs in his bag, Taft was capable on his best day of shooting in the high 80s. He insisted on using the Schenectady Putter, a center-shafted putter that had been banned from tournament play. Taft took the game so seriously that he once canceled a meeting with the president of Chile because it conflicted with a scheduled round of golf. Members of the Myopia Hunt Club in Massachusetts bet $1,000 that Taft could not break 100 on the challenging course. When Taft finished with a 98, he was ecstatic.

President William Howard Taft Courtesy USGA

Despite his portly physique, Taft excelled at golf. On a good day, he could score in the high 80s.

3. JOHN F. KENNEDY

The best golfer ever to occupy the White House was John F. Kennedy, president from 1961 to 1963. Kennedy, who played for the Harvard freshman golf team, was capable of shooting rounds in the 70s. He once shot 36 for 9 holes at the Palm Beach Country Club course. When Kennedy became president, he rarely played golf in public, fearful of the criticism that his predecessor, Dwight Eisenhower, had received.

Kennedy preferred to play in the evening, when the fewest players were on the course. He often skipped holes to avoid contact with the public. Kennedy grimaced when he almost made a hole-in-one, knowing the attention he would receive.

Kennedy was notorious for asking playing partners to concede putts. Once while playing with presidential aide Chris Dunphy at the Seminole Golf Club in North Palm Beach, Florida, Kennedy faced a tricky three-foot putt. Dunphy refused to concede the putt until Kennedy informed him that he was having lunch with the commissioner of the Internal Revenue Service and was discussing whether or not to increase the number of audits of the White House staff.

Because he preferred shorter clubs, Kennedy sometimes played with a woman's set. A set of his golf clubs was auctioned for more than $700,000 during the Jacqueline Kennedy Onassis estate sale.

4. GERALD FORD

Gerald Ford, who occupied the White House from 1974 to 1977, was probably the best athlete of all the presidents. A star football player at the University of Michigan in the early 1930s, Ford was a capable golfer. He once unleashed a 270-yard drive that outdistanced his playing partners, Arnold Palmer and Gary Player.

Ford frequently played in pro-ams and once sank a 40-foot putt during a national golf telecast. He made three holes-in-one, and his career best round was 81. Ford's erratic driving resulted in a few spectators being hit. Bob Hope joked, "Gerald Ford made golf a contact sport."

5. GEORGE BUSH

George Bush, president from 1989 to 1993, inherited his golfing ability from his father, Prescott Bush. Prescott won eight club championships and held Maine's Arundel Golf Club course record with a round of 66. In 1934, Prescott Bush was elected president of the United States Golf Association.

George Bush's maternal grandfather, George Herbert Walker, was also a former president of the USGA and established the Walker Cup, a biannual match between American and British amateur golfers that began in 1922 and continues to this day. George Bush once shot 76, making him one of the best golfers among the presidents. He also defeated Ronald Reagan in a friendly match.

In 1995, Bush played with President Bill Clinton and former president Gerald Ford during the first round of the Bob Hope Chrysler Classic, at Indian Wells, California. Bush defeated Clinton by one shot, with Ford another eight shots back.

6. BILL CLINTON

As a teenager, Bill Clinton caddied for professional Tommy Bolt during a tournament played in Hot Springs, Arkansas. Unlike his predecessor, George Bush, who sometimes played a round of golf in less than two hours, Clinton preferred leisurely rounds that lasted more than five hours.

Clinton twice outdrove Jack Nicklaus in a round at Vail, Colorado. Not averse to taking an occasional mulligan, Clinton has broken 80 in a round. For his forty-ninth birthday, First Lady Hillary Clinton arranged for her husband to play a round with Johnny Miller at the Jackson Hole Golf Club in Wyoming. Miller fired a 69, while Clinton posted a respectable 89.

During a round of golf, it was not unusual for Clinton to be accompanied by several Secret Service agents, a police sniper, and aides carrying nuclear codes and a telephone.

7. WOODROW WILSON

Woodrow Wilson was president from 1913 to 1921. Wilson did not take up golf until his late forties. He usually played six times a week and even used red golf balls so he could play in the snow.

In Wilson's case, practice did not make perfect. He usually scored between 110 and 120 and once carded a 26 on a single hole, the second at the Washington Golf and Country Club Course in Arlington, Virginia. Wilson was on a golf course when he learned of the sinking of the *Lusitania,* and in the morning he asked Congress for the authority to declare war on Germany.

8. RICHARD NIXON

Not blessed with outstanding athletic ability, Richard Nixon became a decent golfer through work and determination. After being criticized while vice president by President Eisenhower for his lack of golfing skills, Nixon improved enough to shoot 84 and defeat Ike in a match.

In September 1961, Nixon used a 6-iron to score a hole-in-one on the third hole at Bel Air Golf Course. He shot 91 for the round, losing a $3 bet with actor Randolph Scott.

As president from 1969 to 1974, Nixon gave golf balls with his name and the presidential seal to his friends as gifts. In 1978, the 65-year-old Nixon broke 80 for the first time.

9. **WARREN HARDING**

Warren Harding, president from 1921 to 1923, played golf in style. Every few holes, he had his butler bring him a tray of glasses of scotch and water. Harding made so many bets during a round that he needed someone to keep track of them all. He usually bet $6 nassaus on the front and back nines and an additional $6 on the match. He made a number of side bets, even on shots in flight. On occasion, he bet against himself. Once while playing poker, Harding lost an entire set of nineteenth-century White House china.

10. **LYNDON JOHNSON**

Lyndon Johnson believed in the adage, If at first you don't succeed, try, try, again. He was known to play up to eight mulligans. President from 1963 to 1969, Johnson might hit a drive 200 yards or top one two feet in front of him.

Johnson once played a round with Dwight Eisenhower. By all accounts, Eisenhower won the first 17 holes. Reporters were on hand to watch the final hole. Johnson rose to the occasion and won the hole with a par. LBJ remarked on his golf game, "I don't have a handicap. I'm all handicap."

All in the Family

Golfing talent often runs in the family. Tom Morris and his son Tom Morris, Jr. combined to win eight British Opens between 1861 and 1872. Harry Vardon and his brother, Tom, finished first and second in the 1903 British Open, played at Prestwick. Senior Tour players Jack Nicklaus and Bob Duval have sons, Gary and David, respectively, on the PGA Tour.

1. THE SMITH BROTHERS

Willie Smith won the 1899 U.S. Open Championship, played at the Baltimore Country Club. His brother, Alex, won the 1906 U.S. Open, played at the Onwentsia Club in Illinois. Willie finished second, seven shots back. At the 1910 U.S. Open, played at the Philadelphia Cricket Club, Alex won his second Open in a three-way playoff with his older brother, Macdonald, and Johnny McDermott. All three brothers were winners of the Western Open.

2. SAM AND J. C. SNEAD

Sam Snead won a record 81 tournaments on the PGA Tour. His nephew, J. C. Snead, joined the tour in 1968 and won

Sam Snead

Though one of the most serious and successful golfers of all time, Sam Snead never forgot the fun of the sport. He liked to joke that he buried all his prize money in tomato cans in his backyard.

eight titles during his career. In 1974, 62-year-old Sam and J. C. Snead teamed to finish second in the Walt Disney World Team Championships.

3. MIKE AND DAVE HILL

Mike Hill won three titles on the PGA Tour, before becoming a star on the Senior Tour. From 1990 to 1992, Hill won 13 tournaments on the Senior Tour. Brother Dave won four Memphis Opens and finished second in the 1970 U.S. Open Championship.

4. THE STOCKTONS

Dave Stockton won 11 tournaments, most notably the PGA championships in 1970 and 1976. In 1994, Stockton and his son, Dave Stockton, Jr., led tournaments on the Senior and PGA tours on the same day. Beginning the final round of the Players Classic Tournament in Dearborn, Michigan, Dave Sr. led by five shots. Dave Jr. was tied for the lead at the Hartford Open. The senior Stockton won the Players Classic by six strokes, while Dave Jr. finished third in the Hartford Open.

5. MARGARET AND HARRIOT CURTIS

At the 1907 U.S. Women's Amateur Championship, played at the Midlothian Country Club in Illinois, Margaret Curtis defeated her sister, Harriot, 7 and 6, to win the title. Harriot had won the championship the previous year.

6. CURT AND TOM BYRUM

Curt and Tom Byrum were the last brothers to win tournaments on the PGA Tour in the same year. In 1989, Curt won the Hardee's Golf Classic and Tom finished first in the Kemper Open.

7. **THE TOOGOODS**

The Toogoods were too good for the competition at the 1956 Tasmanian Open. Peter Toogood won the tournament. His father, Alfred, was second, and his brother, John, finished third.

8. **THE TURNESAS**

Mike Turnesa of Elmsford, New York, had six sons who became professional golfers. One of his sons, Jim, won the 1952 PGA Championship. Willie, the only son who did not turn professional, won the U.S. Amateur Championship in 1938 and 1948.

9. **THE FRIBLEY FAMILY**

In 1971, John Fribley scored a hole-in-one on the seventh hole at the Pana Country Club course in Illinois. His grandson, Scott, also aced the seventh hole four years later. Sixteen years later, Scott's father, Joseph, became the third member of the Fribley family to score a hole-in-one on the same hole.

10. **BARRY AND JODY WOLFE**

In 1990, twin brothers, Barry and Jody Wolfe played a memorable round together at the Scott County Park Course in Gate City, Virginia. On the second hole, the 15-year-olds both used 6-irons to score holes-in-one.

The One and Only

E ach of the following are one-of-a-kind golfing feats.

1. GEORGE LYON

Canadian George Lyon is the only golfer to refuse an Olympic gold medal. Lyon did not take up the game of golf until he was 38 years old. He was 46 when he competed in the 1904 Summer Olympics, in St. Louis. The only competitor not from the United States, Lyon unexpectedly won the gold medal. During the awards ceremony, he walked on his hands. Lyon traveled to the 1908 London Olympics to defend his gold medal. When he arrived, Lyon discovered that he was the lone participant. The British golfers were boycotting the games because of an internal dispute. Officials offered Lyon the gold medal, but he refused to accept it. Golf was discontinued as an Olympic sport following the 1908 Games.

2. BABE DIDRIKSON

Babe Didrikson became the only woman to compete in an all-male tournament on the PGA tour. Didrikson competed in the 1938 Los Angeles Open but missed the cut. At the tournament, she met her future husband, George Zaharias.

3. **BOB CHARLES**

The only left-handed golfer to win a major championship was Bob Charles of New Zealand. In 1963, Charles won the British Open, played at Royal Lytham.

4. **LON HINKLE**

The only golfer to have a tree planted at the U.S. Open Championship to stop him from taking a shortcut was Lon Hinkle. During the first round of the 1979 U.S. Open, played at the Inverness Club in Toledo, Ohio, Hinkle tried an innovative approach to the par-5 eighth hole. Rather than drive down the eighth fairway, Hinkle took a shortcut by driving into the 17th fairway. Tournament officials were not amused and planted a tree overnight to make certain Hinkle played the hole as it was intended to be played. Hale Irwin won the tournament.

5. **ARNOLD MASSY**

Arnold Massy is the only Frenchman to win the British Open. Massy won the 1907 Open, played at Hoylake. Frenchman Jean Van de Velde appeared to be on his way to winning the 1999 British Open until he triple-bogied the final hole and lost in a playoff.

6. **CHICK EVANS, JR.**

The only golfer to compete in 50 consecutive United States Amateur Championships was Chick Evans, Jr. Evans won his first U.S. Amateur Championship in 1907. In 1916, he won both the U.S. Amateur and U.S. Open championships. In 1962, Evans competed in his last U.S. Amateur, at the age of 72.

7. **WILLIE ANDERSON**

Willie Anderson was the only golfer to win the U.S. Open Championship in three consecutive years. Anderson won his first U.S. Open title in 1901. Then he won three straight Opens from 1903 to 1905.

8. **HARRY VARDON**

Only one golfer has won six British Opens. Englishman Harry Vardon won the Open in 1896, 1898, 1899, 1903, 1911, and 1914.

9. **DENIS DURNIAN**

Little-known Denis Durnian set a nine-hole record at the 1983 British Open played at the Royal Birkdale Golf Club. Durnian shot an incredible 28 during the second round. Tom Watson won the tournament, his fifth British Open title.

10. **JO ANN WASHAM**

At the 1979 Women's Kemper Open, played at the Mesa Verde Country Club in Colorado, Jo Ann Washam became the only woman to score two holes-in-one in an LPGA tournament. Washam aced the 16th hole in the second round and scored a second hole-in-one on the 17th hole of the final round.

Bears, Sharks, and Walruses

From "Slammin" Sammy Snead to Lew "The Chin" Worsham, golf has had its share of memorable nicknames.

1. THE GOLDEN BEAR

Jack Nicklaus is generally regarded as the greatest golfer of the twentieth century. Nicklaus's record of 18 major championships is one of golf's most unassailable records. He was nicknamed "The Golden Bear" because of his blond hair and sturdy physique. Early in his career, he had a less favorable nickname. Nicklaus was called "Ohio Fats" by some fans who resented him replacing Arnold Palmer as the game's premier player.

2. THE GREAT WHITE SHARK

Greg Norman is a two-time British Open Champion. The blond Australian got the nickname "The Great White Shark" because of his love of deep-sea fishing. Once while fishing, he shot at some sharks that were chasing the boat.

Craig "The Walrus" Stadler
Stadler's hulking frame and tusk-shaped moustache earned him the affectionate moniker of "The Walrus."

3. **TIGER**

Tiger Woods has dazzled the golf world with his amazing play. Born Eldridge Woods, he was nicknamed "Tiger" at an early age because of his tenacious attitude.

4. **CHAMPAGNE TONY**

Tony Lema was given the nickname "Champagne Tony" when he broke out the bubbly for sportswriters after he won the Orange County Open in 1962. Lema's biggest victory came in the 1964 British Open.

5. **THE WALRUS**

Craig Stadler earned the nickname "The Walrus" because of his stocky build and walrus-like moustache. "The Walrus" won the 1982 Masters and was the PGA tour's leading money winner that year.

6. **FUZZY**

Fuzzy Zoeller was the 1979 Masters champion. His nickname was derived from the initials of his name, Frank Urban Zoeller.

7. **THE ICEMAN**

One of golf's most accomplished players, Ben Hogan won nine major tournaments, including four U.S. Open Championship titles. Known for his aloof nature, Hogan was called "The Iceman" by British fans. The Scots called Hogan "The Wee Ice Man."

8. **GENE THE MACHINE**

Gene Littler won the 1961 U.S. Open Championship. He was nicknamed "Gene the Machine" because of his effortless swing and mechanical approach to the game.

9. **SUPERMEX**

Lee Trevino was nicknamed "Supermex" because of his Mexican-American heritage. He lived up to his nickname by winning two United States Opens, two British Opens, and two PGA tournaments.

10. **LORD BYRON**

Byron Nelson dominated golf over a two-year span from 1945 to 1946. During that time, Nelson won an incredible 26 tournaments. He was nicknamed "Lord Byron" because he was the Lord of the Links. The original Lord Byron was a renowned nineteenth-century poet.

Muffin Face and the Moon Man

Not every golfer's nickname is as catchy as "The Golden Bear."

1. THE MOON MAN

Kermit Zarley won the 1970 Canadian Open, but he got more attention for his unusual name. Bob Hope said, "It sounds as he's the pro from the moon." After Hope's remark, Zarley became known as "The Moon Man."

2. MUFFIN FACE

One of the most unflattering golf nicknames belonged to Bobby Locke. The South African, one of the greatest putters in golf history, was the winner of four British Opens between 1949 and 1957. Locke was called "Muffin Face" because of his lack of expression while playing.

3. THE DIAMOND MAN

Calvin Peete broke his left elbow as a child, leaving him unable to straighten his arm. Peete did not take up golf until he was 23 years old. Despite his physical handicap, he won 11 tournaments between 1982 and 1986 and led the PGA Tour in driving accuracy for 10 consecutive years. Peete was nicknamed "The Diamond Man" because he had once sold jewelry and had diamonds inlaid in his front teeth.

4. DISCO DUCK

Richard Zokol was nicknamed "Disco Duck" because he wore headphones on the course during the 1982 Greater Milwaukee Open. Ten years later, Zokol won the Milwaukee Open.

5. RADAR

Mike Reid's biggest victory came in the 1988 NEC World Series of Golf. He was known as "Radar" because of his incredible accuracy off the tee.

6. JUG

Arnold McSpaden won the 1939 Canadian Open. That year, he shot a 59 in a practice round for the Texas Open. It would be another 38 years before another player broke 60 in a PGA tournament. McSpaden was nicknamed "Jug" because of the prominent dimple in his jaw.

7. CAR PARK GOLFER

Seve Ballesteros won three British Opens and a pair of Masters titles. The Spaniard is one of golf's best scramblers. His frequent errant drives earned him the nickname "The Car Park Golfer."

8. **LUMPY**

Tim Herron is one of the longest drivers on the PGA Tour. He is known as "Lumpy" because of his ample physique.

9. **THE CHOCOLATE SOLDIER**

Henry Picard won 26 tournaments during his career. He got the nickname "The Chocolate Soldier" because he made his professional debut at the Hershey Country Club. Hershey, Pennsylvania, is one of the largest chocolate-manufacturing centers in the world.

10. **LEAKY**

Bruce Lietzke won more than a dozen tournaments, including the 1981 Bob Hope and Byron Nelson Classics. Lietzke was nicknamed "Leaky" after the name of his boat.

Teed Off

In 1900, Rhoda Adair won the British and Irish Ladies Long Driving Championship in Lancashire, England, with a modest drive of 173 yards. Meet some of golf's longest hitters.

1. HARRY LEACH

On May 26, 1954, Harry Leach teed off on the first hole of the Old St. Andrews Course in Scotland. His drive flew out of bounds and landed in a construction truck on its way to the local dump. Leach's ball ended up in a pile of trash more than a mile away from the course.

2. NILS LIED

John Daly routinely drives a golf ball 300 yards, but Nils Lied hit a drive that traveled 2,640 yards. In 1962, the Australian meteorologist drove the ball on a sheet of ice at Mawson Base, Antarctica. By the time the ball stopped on the slick surface, it had traveled a mile and a half.

3. JOHN DALY

In 1991, John Daly drove a golf ball on a runway of the Denver airport. The drive flew 360 yards in the air and rolled an additional 450 yards.

4. CARL COOPER

Carl Cooper hit a drive that came to rest more than 300 yards past the hole. Cooper's monster drive occurred on the 450-yard third hole of the Oak Hills Country Club in San Antonio during the 1952 H.E.B. Texas Open. His drive landed on a cart path and skipped past the third green. The ball kept rolling downhill until it came to rest near the 12th green. Cooper's drive measured an incredible 787 yards.

5. HELEN DOBSON

Helen Dobson proved that men were not the only golfers capable of long drives. On October 31, 1987, Dobson launched a drive 531 yards at RAF Honington, England.

6. MICHAEL AUSTIN

Sixty-four-year-old Michael Austin hit a drive to remember during the 1974 U.S. National Seniors' Championship, played at the Winterwood Golf Course in Las Vegas, Nevada. Austin's historic drive took place on the 450-yard fifth hole. With a 35-mile-per-hour wind at his back, Austin drove the ball within a yard of the pin, where it then bounced off the green and rolled 65 yards past the flagstick.

7. GEORGE BAYER

During a tournament in Las Vegas in 1948, George Bayer hit a mammoth drive on a 476-yard hole. The ball hit a spectator standing 30 yards behind the green.

8. ARNOLD PALMER

In 1977, Arnold Palmer drove a ball from the second stage at the Eiffel Tower, 300 feet above the streets of Paris. The drive bounced into the second deck of a double-decker bus, more than 400 yards from the base of the tower.

9. JIM DENT

In 1992, Jim Dent led the Senior Tour in driving distance with an average of 283 yards per drive. The 53-year-old averaged the same distance as John Daly, who led the PGA Tour.

10. CRAIG WOOD

Craig Wood hit the longest drive in British Open history during the 1933 tournament, played at the Old St. Andrews Course in Scotland. Aided by a strong tailwind off the Firth of Forth, Wood's drive on the fifth hole traveled 430 yards. Wood finished second in the Open, behind winner Denny Shute.

Driving You Nuts

When a player drives a golf ball, there is no telling where it will land.

1. MATHIEU BOYA

Mathieu Boya lived in the small African country Benin. Because Benin did not have a golf course, Boya practiced hitting golf balls in a field next to the Benin Air Base. In 1987, Boya hit a drive that was responsible for destroying the entire Benin Air Force. His drive struck a bird flying over the airport. The disabled bird then fell into the open cockpit of a fighter jet attempting to take off, causing the pilot to lose control and crash into four Mirage jets parked on the runway. All five planes, valued at more than $40 million, were destroyed. Boya was jailed and told he would be released once he was able to repay the damages.

2. GEORGE RUSSELL

Most golfers would be happy with a 300-yard drive, but not George Russell. Playing in the 1913 Braids Tournament in Scotland, Russell teed off on an elevated tee. He hit the ball on his backswing, and the ball rolled down a steep hill behind the tee. Russell became the only golfer to hit a drive 300 yards—backward.

3. COW CHIP OPEN

The Cow Chip Open was played annually in Lawrence, Nebraska. More than 50 cows grazed on the course, leaving cow pies everywhere. In 1965, a player from Chicago, who preferred to remain anonymous, hit a low drive that struck a hardened cow chip, causing the ball to rebound 10 yards behind the tee. The golfer, who was only one over at the time, shot an 11 on the hole.

4. MARK WITT

Mark Witt decided to try to drive the ball onto the green of the 300-yard par-4 17th hole at the Willow Creek Country Club during the 1991 Ben Hogan Knoxville Open. The drive carried 300 yards and bounced onto a road adjacent to the fairway. To Witt's horror, the ball began rolling back down the road. It continued to roll back 250 yards and stopped only 50 yards from the tee. Instead of a possible birdie, Witt settled for a bogey.

5. AUBREY BOOMER

In 1923, Aubrey Boomer hit a drive at the St. Annes Golf Course in Scotland that went straight up in the air. Incredibly, the ball landed in his right-hand pocket.

6. LEE BARON

On the 13th hole of the Rainbow Canyon Resort Course in Temecula, California, Lee Baron popped up his drive, causing the ball to strike him in the back. He was struck in the back by his own drive.

7. OTIS GUERNSEY

When Otis Guernsey teed off from the ninth hole at the Apawanis Golf Club in Rye, New York, he shanked the ball, causing it to land on the 11th green of the adjoining Green Meadows Golf Course located in Harrison, New York. His errant drive had landed on another golf course, in another city.

8. JOE KIRKWOOD

Joe Kirkwood was an Australian trick shot artist during the 1930s. One of his favorite shots was to use his comely assistant as a tee. He would have her lie down on her back with a Hershey Kiss in her mouth. Kirkwood then would tee the ball on top of the candy and drive it without harming the assistant. After the trick shot was completed, Kirkwood would dramatically kiss her.

9. GEORGE ASHDOWN

George Ashdown, a club professional from Esther, England, played an entire round on November 23, 1931, with a human tee. He hit all 18 drives off a rubber tee strapped on the forehead of a female assistant.

10. G. S. WILLIAMS, JR.

On January 22, 1989, G. S. Williams, Jr. hit a golf ball from the top of Aconcagua Mountain in Argentina. The peak was 22,834 feet above sea level.

Putting Around

Everyone has his or her own unique putting style. Golfers use putters of varying lengths and blades. These golfers had memorable experiences with their putter.

1. BOBBY LOCKE

South African Bobby Locke was considered the greatest putter in golf history. Locke's fantastic putting helped him win the British Open in 1949, 1950, 1952, and 1957. In 1945, Locke did not three-putt a single green, despite playing nearly 1,800 holes of golf. Locke was so fond of his putter that he sometimes slept with it.

2. CHICK EVANS

Chick Evans won two U.S. Amateur and one U.S. Open Championships. Evans sometimes carried four putters in his golf bag, each one designed for various green conditions.

3. NOTAH BEGAY III

A former Stanford teammate of Tiger Woods, Notah Begay made his own mark in 1999 with victories in the Reno-Tahoe

Open and Michelob Championship in his rookie season on the PGA Tour. Begay putts the ball both left- and right-handed, depending on which way the ball will break.

4. LEO DIEGEL

Leo Diegel won 29 tournaments and was the PGA Champion in 1928 and 1929. Plagued by a bad case of nerves, Diegel employed an unusual putting style. He stood with elbows out, legs wide apart, and the shaft of the putter under his chin. At the 1933 British Open, Diegel whiffed a two-foot putt that cost him a chance to be in a playoff with Denny Shute and Craig Wood.

5. HALE IRWIN

Hale Irwin's careless attempt at a putt cost him a chance to win the 1983 British Open, played at Royal Birkdale. During the third round, Irwin whiffed a two-inch tap-in when he carelessly let his putter hit the ground, causing it to bounce over the ball. It was a costly mistake—Irwin finished one shot behind winner Tom Watson.

6. ANDREW KIRKALDY

Andrew Kirkaldy would have been the 1889 British Open champion had he not missed a one-inch putt. Playing the 14th hole of the Musselburgh Golf Course in Scotland, Kirkaldy whiffed an easy tap-in and lost the Open in a play-off with Willie Park, Jr.

7. HARRY VARDON

Harry Vardon won the 1900 U.S. Open Championship, played at the Chicago Golf Club. However, he finished the tournament on an embarrassing note when he whiffed a one-inch tap-in on the final hole.

8. BRIAN BARNES

Englishman Brian Barnes was in contention during the second round of the 1968 French Open, played at Saint Cloud, when disaster struck. Barnes lost control after missing a three-foot par putt on the eighth hole. After lipping out, he tried to rake the ball into the hole. Frustrated, he began batting the ball back and forth. It took him 12 strokes before he finally holed out.

9. CHICK CHATTEN

Chick Chatten required only 16 putts during a round played at the Elks Country Club Course on August 31, 1952. He one-putted 14 greens, had one two-putt, and chipped in on three holes.

10. KENNY KNOX

The record for the fewest putts on a 72-hole tournament on the PGA Tour was set by Kenny Knox at the 1989 MCI Heritage Classic, played at the Harbour Town Golf Links in Hilton Head Island, South Carolina. He needed only 93 putts for the four rounds. Despite Knox's putting heroics, the tournament was won by Payne Stewart, with a score of 268.

Spoons, Mashies, and Niblicks

One of the major ways golf has changed over the years is the improvement in equipment. The wooden-shafted clubs of bygone days have been replaced by lightweight space-age metals.

1. WOOD-SHAFTED CLUBS

Early golf clubs were given names such as brassies, spoons, cleeks, lofters, mashies, and niblicks. The shafts were made from ash, hickory, or hazel. The club heads were usually carved from apple, beech, or thorn woods. With the advent of the harder gutta-percha ball, which damaged these softer woods, persimmon was substituted. The wooden-shafted clubs remained in vogue until the early twentieth century.

2. FEATHER BALL

The feather ball was used during the early nineteenth century. The ball was generally filled with goose feathers. The lightweight ball lost its shape after repeated use and sometimes broke apart. The feather ball did not travel nearly as far as the modern wound ball. In 1836, Samuel Messieux, aided by a strong tailwind, set a record by driving a feather ball 361 yards on the 14th hole at the Old St. Andrews Golf Course.

3. GUTTA-PERCHA BALL

In the 1850s, the feather ball was replaced by the gutta-percha ball. In 1845, Robert Paterson used gutta-percha, a rubber-like substance made from the sap of a tropical tree, to resole his shoes. When the substance came off his shoes, he molded it into a golf ball and played a few holes. He discovered that the gutta-percha ball outdistanced the feather ball, which was the standard of the day. Within a decade, the gutta-percha ball was the ball of choice for golfers.

4. PNEUMATIC BALL

In 1905, the pneumatic ball was developed by the B.F. Goodrich Company. The rubber ball was filled with compressed air. The pneumatic ball appeared to be the ball of the future when Arthur Smith shot a record score of 278 to win the 1905 Western Open, played at the Cincinnati Country Club. Unfortunately, it was soon discovered that the pneumatic ball had a tendency to explode in hot weather, and it was soon no longer in use.

5. PHOSPHORESCENT PAINT

In the late 1890s, P. G. Tait, a mathematics professor at Edinburgh University, played up to five rounds a day at St. Andrews. Tait arranged a nighttime match with the famed scientist Thomas Henry Huxley and Professor Crum Brown. Tait painted the golf balls with phosphorescent paint. The match ended prematurely when Professor Brown's glove, ignited by the flammable paint, caught fire and burned his hand.

6. **FOUR-SIDED PUTTER**

During the early 1900s, William Davis, a New Jersey inventor, created a four-sided putter. The curious invention never caught on with golfers.

7. **RUT IRON**

There were a number of specialty clubs in the early days of golf. One of the strangest was the rut iron, a club designed to hit balls out of ruts caused by wagon wheels.

8. **SOUND-EMITTING BALL**

In 1937, Englishman Sir J. Simon invented a golf ball that emitted a sound so that it could be located. Although the invention seemed to be a godsend for duffers, the sound-emitting golf ball has not been heard from for decades.

9. **ELECTRONIC PUTTER**

In 1938, Professor A. M. Low invented a putter that lit up when the club was swung correctly. The electronic putter, while an ingenious invention, did not revolutionize putting.

10. **MECHANIZED CLUB**

In 1942, the mechanized club was patented. The club applauded the golfer for a good swing and gave a raspberry for a flawed one.

Not Playing with a Full Bag

In the 1930s, the number of clubs in a bag was limited to 14 in an attempt to ensure that more prosperous golfers did not have an unfair advantage. Until that time, golfers carried as many as 30 clubs in their bags. The following golfers did not use standard equipment.

1. **THAD DABER**

The winner of the 1987 World One-Club Championship in Cary, North Carolina, was Thad Daber. Each competitor was permitted to use only one club during his round on the Lochmere Golf Club Course. Daber shot a 70 using only a 6-iron.

2. **JOHN HUMM**

John Humm of Long Island, New York, once shot a 34 for nine holes using only a 3-iron. The next day, he played the same nine with a full set of clubs and shot a 40.

3. SAM SNEAD

During World War II, golf balls were scarce and expensive because of the shortage of rubber. At the 1945 Los Angeles Open, Sam Snead used only one golf ball during the tournament. The ball had been given to him by Bing Crosby. By the final round, the cover of the ball was loose, but Snead still managed to win the tournament.

4. GLORIA MINOPRIO

Gloria Minoprio was a competitor in the English Ladies' championships during the 1930s. She carried only two clubs in her bag, a 2-iron and a spare 2-iron. Although she never won the championship, she did occasionally win matches despite her limited club selection.

5. CURTIS STRANGE

Curtis Strange won back-to-back United States Open Championships in 1988 and 1989, but his most exasperating moment on the tour occurred at the 1979 Jackie Gleason-Inverrary Classic in Florida. Strange's caddie, Mark Freiburg, lost his balance while crossing a bridge leading to the ninth tee. Strange prevented his caddie from falling, but most of his golf clubs disappeared into the water. He was forced to complete the round with four clubs, three irons and a putter. A diver recovered his clubs before the next round.

6. BARB THOMAS

Disgusted with her play, Barb Thomas threw away her putter after the ninth hole during a round at the 1986 Konica San Jose Classic. On the back nine Thomas putted with her long irons. Thomas shot 42 on the front nine with her putter and 43 on the back nine without it.

7. **CHICK EVANS**

At the 1916 U.S. Open Championships played at the Minkahola Golf Club in Minneapolis, Minnesota, Chick Evans's winning score of 286 set a record that lasted 20 years. Evans used only six clubs in his record-setting effort.

8. **JOHN BALL**

In 1907, John Ball came up with an ingenious solution to win a bet. A dense fog made play nearly impossible at the Hoylake Golf Course in Cheshire, England. Ball bet he could break 90 without losing a ball. He won the wager with a round of 81 by using a black ball, which was easier to locate in the fog.

9. **LEO DIEGEL**

Leo Diegel won the Canadian Open four times during his career. The eccentric golfer carried four different drivers in his bag. One of the clubs was used to slice the ball, another only when a hook was needed, and the other two for various wind conditions.

10. **LAWSON LITTLE**

The highlight of Lawson Little's career was a victory in the 1940 U.S. Open Championship, played at the Canterbury Golf Club in Cleveland, Ohio. Early in his career Little carried as many as 30 clubs in his bag, twice the current limit.

Fishing Rods and Buckshot Balls

Most golfers play the game with a set of clubs and a golf ball. As the next list demonstrates, innovative golfers have played the game with unorthodox equipment.

1. ARCHIE COMPSTON

Archie Compston was an outstanding English golfer during the 1920s. He had the eccentric habit of having three caddies accompany him during a round. One caddie performed the normal duty of carrying his clubs. A second caddie's only job was to carry Compston's apparel. And the third caddie brought along cigarettes, cigars, and pipes for the chain-smoking golfer.

2. J. J. MACKINLAY

J. J. MacKinlay used a fishing rod to play a round of golf in Wellington, England, in 1913. MacKinlay attached a 25-ounce weight to a fishing rod and cast it around the course. He needed 102 casts to complete the 18 holes.

3. WILLIE HAMMOND

On May 27, 1928, aerial golf made its debut at The Westbury Golf Club in New York. The purpose of the game was to drop a golf ball from an airplane. The player whose ball landed closest to the pin won the hole. A team captained by Willie Hammond won the match by three holes.

4. F. M. WEBSTER

F. M. Webster challenged golfer Harry Vardon to a one-of-a-kind match in 1913. Instead of hitting a golf ball, Webster threw a javelin. To complete a hole, Webster was required to throw his javelin within two feet of the hole. Vardon won the match 5 holes to 4.

5. JOE FLYNN

Joe Flynn did not need clubs to play a round of golf. Flynn threw the golf ball around the course. He set a record on March 27, 1975, by needing only 82 throws to play 18 holes at Bermuda's Port Royal Golf Course.

6. RUDOLPH TIMMERMAN

Most golfers toss golf clubs in anger, but Rudolph Timmerman won competitions doing it. At the 1936 Club Throwing Tournament at the Druid Hills Country Club in Atlanta, Timmerman set a record by tossing a club 61 yards.

7. MAITLAND DOUGAL

The weather was horrible for the 1860 Autumn Medal Competition at St. Andrews, Scotland. Gale-force winds made playing conditions nearly unplayable. The wind was so strong that ships were being grounded. Captain Maitland

Dougal spent five hours trying to keep his ship off the rocks. Afterward, he competed in the tournament. Dougal drilled a hole in his gutta-percha ball and filled it with buckshot to make it heavier so it would not be blown off course by the wind. Dougal shot 112, to finish second, eight shots behind winner William Thompson.

8. **A. A. HORNE**

Golf balls were scarce during World War II, because of the rationing of rubber. Some players were forced to play with wooden golf balls. A. A. Horne won a Wooden Golf Ball tournament played in Potchefstroom, South Africa. His winning score for 18 holes was 90.

9. **SEBASTIAN MIGUEL**

Sebastian Miguel of Spain is the only golfer to use yellow driving-range balls during a tournament. He was playing in the Portuguese Open when he hit 22 balls out of bounds on the 13th hole. When he ran out of balls, he had to borrow a yellow driving-range ball from a playing partner in order to finish the round. In 1959, Miguel redeemed himself by winning the Portuguese Open.

10. **BILL KRATZERT**

Bill Kratzert was forced to withdraw from the 1986 Anheuser Busch Golf Classic in Williamsburg, Virginia, because he ran out of golf balls. It was a hot July day and Kratzert's caddie decided to lighten the bag he was carrying by bringing fewer balls. After Kratzert lost three balls during the round, he discovered there were no more in the bag and walked off the course.

Nothing to Knicker At

During a round of golf, Lyndon Johnson complimented evangelist Billy Graham on his yellow pigskin golf shoes. Graham responded by sending the president six pairs of the yellow shoes. These golfers stood out on the golf course by what they wore or did not wear.

1. PAYNE STEWART

Payne Stewart was the fashion plate of the PGA Tour. He wore knickers which paid homage to a bygone era in golf. He sometimes played in outfits that matched the colors of the uniforms of his favorite National Football League teams. In 1988, Stewart played in an exhibition at the Hercules Country Club in Wilmington, Delaware. He made a wager with three women professional golfers that he could beat their best ball. If he won, the women would have to remove their shorts. If he lost, Stewart would agree to remove his trademark knickers. Stewart lost the match on the final hole and removed his knickers, to the amusement of the women golfers and spectators.

2. **TOPLESS DANCERS**

From 1990 to 1992, a golf tournament was played at the Forest Creek Golf Course in Round Rock, Texas. Sponsored by nightclubs in Austin, it featured topless dancers who wore only bikini bottoms. The exotic dancers drove golf carts and delivered refreshments to the competitors, who were understandably distracted by the sight.

3. **IAN BAKER-FINCH**

Ian Baker-Finch, the 1991 British Open Champion, showed more than his golf game during the 1993 Colonial Invitational. On the 13th hole, he hit his ball into the edge of a pond. Baker-Finch took off his shoes and socks, then shocked spectators by removing his pants, in order to keep them dry. Wearing only his boxer shorts, he hit the ball 12 feet past the hole and missed the putt for a bogey 4.

4. **GERALD MOXOM**

Gerald Moxom decided to play a round of golf following his wedding in 1934. Dressed in his wedding suit, Moxom shot a 61 on the West Hill Course in Surrey, England.

5. **KING HASSAN II**

King Hassan II of Morocco loved golf so much that he built a nine-hole course on the grounds of his palace. He sponsored a pro-am event in which he played. The king insisted on playing with three sets of clubs. He had a building constructed next to the first tee that housed more than 100 pairs of golf shoes, so that no matter what outfit the king decided to wear, his shoes would be color coordinated.

6. **SLAM INVITATIONAL**

The SLAM Invitational, played in New Orleans, was part golf tournament, part costume party. Competitors were encouraged to dress in outrageous outfits. Each team consisted of a man and a woman. The winning man was awarded a tattered green jacket, and the victorious woman was given a vinyl handbag.

7. **NIGEL FARRAR**

In 1914, English soldier Nigel Farrar made a bet that he could break 100 while wearing his military uniform. Dressed in full military gear, Farrar shot 94 at the Royston Links Golf Course.

8. **GENE SARAZEN**

On the night before an exhibition match with Walter Hagen in 1922, Gene Sarazen was sent an orange tie along with a letter from a Ziegfeld Follies showgirl. The note wished Sarazen good luck in his match with Hagen. The next day, Sarazen wore the tie. During the match, he kept looking into the gallery to see if he could recognize his secret admirer. As a result, his game suffered. Late in the round, Hagen asked Sarazen where he got the tie. At that moment, Sarazen realized that it was Hagen, the master of mind games, who had sent him the tie.

9. **SAM SNEAD**

Sam Snead always considered himself a country boy. During a practice round at the 1942 Masters, Snead played barefoot. Byron Nelson won the tournament. However, Snead did win Masters titles in 1949, 1952, and 1954.

Gene Sarazen and Ben Hogan

Courtesy USGA

Though they squared off in many PGA tournaments, Hogan and Sarazen maintained a friendship on and off the course.

10. **MARK WIEBE**

The PGA Tour has a rule that does not permit golfers to wear shorts. At the 1992 Anheuser Busch Classic in Williamsburg, Virginia, the temperature reached 102 degrees. Golfer Mark Wiebe defied the ban and wore shorts on the practice tee. Wiebe was fined $500 for his indiscretion.

Play the Ball Where It Lies

A t the 1987 Tournament Players Championship, Raymond Floyd hit a shot that landed in his golf bag. Playing in the Southern Amateur Tournament in New Orleans, Bobby Jones hit a shot that landed in a shoe resting in a wheelbarrow. Phil Rodgers cost himself a chance to win the 1962 U.S. Open Championship by taking four shots to hit out of a tree. Here are some more incredible unplayable lies.

1. SAM SNEAD

While playing in the Cleveland Open, Sam Snead hit a shot through the open door of the men's locker room, and the ball rolled into the men's bathroom. Snead was penalized two shots and lost the tournament by one stroke.

2. HALE IRWIN

At the 1973 Sea Pines Heritage Classic played in Hilton Head, South Carolina, Hale Irwin hit a shot that struck a female spectator in the chest, and the ball lodged in her brassiere. An official advised the woman to remove the ball from her brassiere, and Irwin was given a free drop.

3. NIGEL DENHAM

Nigel Denham was not bothered by an unplayable lie he experienced at the 1974 English Amateur Strokeplay Championship, played at The Moortown Golf Club. One of his approach shots bounced through the green and rolled into the open door of the clubhouse bar. Undeterred, Denham chipped through the bar window to within 12 feet of the hole.

4. OSCAR GRIMES

Oscar Grimes hit a money shot at the 1939 Western Open qualifier. His shot went out of bounds and landed in the open drawer of a cash register at a hamburger stand.

5. CURTIS SIFFORD

Curtis Sifford hit a shot at the Quad Cities Open in Iowa that landed in a hot dog left by a spectator. Sifford wiped the mustard off the ball and hit the next shot onto the green.

6. MRS. BLACKFORD

A golfer from Crawfordsville, Indiana, identified as Mrs. Blackford, hit a shot that landed in a tree during a round she played on August 26, 1923. After climbing the tree, she discovered that the ball had come to rest in a bird's nest. Amazingly, she chipped the ball onto the green and sank her putt for a par.

7. CARY MIDDLECOFF

Two-time U.S. Open Championship winner Cary Middlecoff lost a tournament because a spectator threw his ball into the rough. The mishap occurred during the 1952 Palm Beach

Round Robin Tournament, at the Wykagyl Country Club in New Rochelle, New York. On the 16th hole, Middlecoff was leading the tournament when he hit a shot that landed in the pocket of a spectator. The fan, confused by the situation, tossed the ball into the rough and ran away. Middlecoff double-bogeyed the hole and lost the tournament.

8. **HARRY BRADSHAW**

Harry Bradshaw lost the 1949 British Open because a shot he hit on the fifth hole of the Royal St. George's Course in Sandwich, England, landed in a broken beer bottle. When his drive landed in the bottle, he decided to play it. Bradshaw advanced the shot only 25 yards and scored a double-bogey on the hole. The hole proved costly—he lost a playoff with Bobby Locke.

9. **C. H. ALISON**

In 1904, C. H. Alison was involved in a tight match at the Woking Golf Course in England. Alison's approach shot landed on the roof of the clubhouse. He calmly climbed a ladder and hit a shot that landed on the green. The incredible shot enabled him to halve the hole.

10. **BOBBY LOCKE**

During the 1936 Irish Open, Bobby Locke hit a shot on the 12th hole of the Royal Dublin Course that headed straight for the pin. He walked to the green but could not locate the ball. To his amazement, Locke discovered that the ball had lodged in the flag. It fell to the ground when he removed the stick, and Locke made the short putt for a birdie 2.

Believe-It-Or-nots

I n golf anything can happen.

1. MONICA HANNAH

Despite being nine months pregnant, Monica Hannah entered the 1993 Greater Cincinnati Women's Amateur Championship. She endured 90-degree temperatures to advance to the final match against defending champion Louise Kepley. Hannah, who was due to have her baby any day, prevailed 2 and 1 to win the championship.

2. DR. ALCORN

In 1928, Dr. Alcorn of Wentworth Falls, Australia, hit a shot that he could never repeat in a million years. His approach shot struck another ball hit by another golfer playing from the other side of the fairway. The balls both fell into the cup, recording a birdie for each player.

3. JIMMY HINES

Jimmy Hines gave Sam Snead an unexpected break during the 1938 PGA Championship, played in Shawnee-on-Delaware, Pennsylvania. Snead's ball was already on the green when Hines hit a chip shot. The ball hit Snead's ball and both rolled into the cup for birdie 2s.

4. MARK CALCAVECCHIA

Life played a dirty trick on Mark Calcavecchia at the 1986 Kemper Open, played at the TPC Avenel Course in Potomac, Maryland, when he drove a ball into a ravine. While climbing down the hill, he fell into a large mud puddle. Covered with mud, Calcavecchia was forced to withdraw from the tournament.

5. JIM ENGLAND

In 1976, Jim England played nine holes at the Chapparal Country Club in Bullhead City, Arizona, while blindfolded. Using only a 5-iron, an 8-iron, and a putter, England shot 46. The next day, playing without the blindfold and with a full set of clubs, he shot 48.

6. BOBBY JONES

Bobby Jones went into the final round of the 1926 British Open in second place. On arrival at the Royal Lytham and St. Annes Golf Club, he realized that he had left his player's badge at the hotel. Although he was one of the most famous golfers in the world, the security guard refused to let him in without identification. Jones had to buy a ticket to gain admission to the course. Unshaken by his ordeal, Jones won his first British Open.

7. **BOB HUDSON**

Bob Hudson made golf history by scoring consecutive holes-in-one during a tournament. He achieved the feat during the 1971 Martini International Tournament in Norwich, England. During the second round, Hudson aced the 11th and 12th holes.

8. **JOHN DRUMMOND**

During the summer, it does not get dark in Iceland. The Arctic Open, played in Iceland, holds the distinction of being the only tournament played after midnight. A playoff for the 1992 Arctic Open Championship did not conclude until 4:30 A.M. The winner was British professional John Drummond.

9. **FULTON ALLEM**

Before he won his first event on the South African Tour, Fulton Allem finished runner-up 18 times. Following his initial victory, Allem became a consistent winner in South Africa during the 1980s, including the 1988 Sun City Million Dollar Challenge. Three years later, he won his first tournament on the PGA Tour, the 1991 Independent Insurance Agent Open.

10. **OSCAR MCCASH, JR.**

The double eagle is the rarest score in golf. Oscar McCash, Jr. scored double eagles twice on the same hole—on the same day. In 1983, McCash scored double eagle 2s during morning and afternoon rounds on the 471-yard eighth hole at the Decatur Country Club in Texas.

Making the Rounds

These are not your average rounds of golf.

1. HARRY DEARTH

Harry Dearth bet that he could win a match while clad in a suit of armor. The 1912 match took place at Bushey Hall in England. Dearth played well, but lost the match 2 and 1.

2. HENRY HOWELL

In 1926, Henry Howell bet that he could shoot a round of 65 or better in less than 70 minutes. Offered odds of 40 to 1, Howell shot a 63 on the Glamorganshire Golf Club Course in England. He finished the outstanding round in just 68 minutes to win the bet.

3. DICK HARDISON

On July 21, 1984, 61-year-old Dick Hardison fired a round of 68 at the Sea Mountain Golf Course in Punaluu, Hawaii. What made his round even more amazing was that it was completed in only 49 minutes.

4. JAMES CARVILL

If you see James Carvill on a course, you had better let him play through. On June 18, 1987, Carvill completed the fastest round in golf history. He played 18 holes at the Warrenpoint Golf Club in Down, Ireland, in just 27 minutes.

5. LADDIE LUCAS

Laddie Lucas proved that not seeing is believing. On August 7, 1954, Lucas shot a round of 87 while blindfolded at the Sandy Lodge Golf Course in Hertfordshire, England.

6. WILLIAM INGLE

William Ingle scored a hole-in-one on the first hole of the Torphin Golf Course in Scotland on September 2, 1920. He began his round with scores of 1, 2, 3, 4, and 5. Had the progression continued throughout the round, his final score would have been 171.

7. RONALD JONES

Ronald Jones finished his July 1934 round at the Addington Palace Golf Course in England with a flourish. He eagled the 17th hole by holing his approach shot from the fairway. Jones aced the 18th hole, a challenging 234-yard par 3. For the final five holes, Jones scored 5, 4, 3, 2, and 1.

8. R. H. CORBETT

R. H. Corbett had an easy time checking his scorecard at the 1916 Tangye Cup in Mullim, England. He scored 3 on nine consecutive holes. His nine-hole score of 27 featured two eagles, four birdies, and three pars.

9. **DAVE STRUTH**

In 1876, Dave Struth shot a round of 93 at the Old St. Andrews Course in Scotland. What made the round noteworthy was that it was played at night, by the light of the moon.

10. **CHICK EVANS**

Before the final round of the 1991 Vantage Championship at Tanglewood Park Golf Course in Clemmons, North Carolina, senior player Chick Evans injured his right arm, forcing him to play the entire round with a 7-iron. Evans finished the painful round with a score of 126.

Aces in the Hole

For most golfers, a hole-in-one is the ultimate accomplishment. Most players spend their entire lives without scoring an ace. For other golfers, holes-in-one are almost commonplace. In 1966, husband and wife Harold and Ginny Leyes scored holes-in-one on the same hole during a round in South Bend, Indiana. In September 1974, Douglas Porteous scored four holes-in-one over a 39-hole span in Glasgow, Scotland. That same year, Robert Taylor aced the same hole three days in a row in Norfolk, England.

1. JOSEPH HARRIS

Joseph Harris spent a lifetime playing the Pines Par-3 Golf Course in Hollywood, Florida. Using only a putter, Harris aced an incredible 168 holes. Ironically, putting was the weak point of his game.

2. SCOTT PALMER

Scott Palmer holds many records for holes-in-one. He recorded more than 100 aces, including 33 during a period from

June 1983 to June 1984. Palmer also had holes-in-one during four consecutive rounds in October 1983.

3. NORMAN MANLEY

Norman Manley recorded more than 50 holes-in-one. His greatest achievement was scoring aces on two successive par-4 holes on September 2, 1964. The golfing rarity took place on the seventh and eighth holes of the Del Valle Country Club Course in Saugus, California.

4. ART WALL, JR.

Art Wall, Jr., the 1959 Masters champion, holds the record for holes-in-one by a professional. Wall scored 42 holes-in-one between 1936 and 1979.

5. JOSEPH BOYDSTONE

The only golfer to make three holes-in-one on a front nine was Joseph Boydstone. He aced the third, fourth, and ninth holes at the Bakersfield Golf Club in California, on October 10, 1962.

6. HAROLD SNIDER

Seventy-five-year-old Harold Snider scored a hole-in-one on the eighth hole of the Ironwood Golf Course in Phoenix, Arizona, on June 9, 1976. Snider proved it was no fluke by also recording holes-in-one on the 13th and 14th holes.

7. BERNARD BURKETT

Bernard Burkett scored six holes-in-one over a 43-year period. His aces occurred in 1937, 1950, 1958, 1961, 1971, and 1980.

8. **JOE LUCIUS**

On May 12, 1984, Joe Lucius scored a hole-in-one on the 15th hole at the Mohawk Golf Club in Tiffin, Ohio. It marked the thirteenth time he had aced that same hole. Lucius had had 10 holes-in-one on the 10th hole.

9. **MRS. PADDY MARTIN**

Mrs. Paddy Martin scored a hole-in-one on the third hole of the Rickmansworth Golf Course in England on Good Friday 1960. The following day she aced the same 125-yard hole. Two days later, her tee shot once again found the bottom of the cup. Incredibly, she had scored three holes-in-one on the same hole in a four-day span.

10. **GORDON TAYLOR**

In 1906, Gordon Taylor scored a hole-in-one on the sixth hole of the Royal Dornoch Golf Course in Cape Town, South Africa. Fifty-five years later, he scored his second hole-in-one on the 17th hole of the Royal Cape Golf Course.

not-So-Easy Aces

Each of these golfers experienced one-of-a-kind holes-in-one.

1. ARTHUR POWELL

Arthur Powell of Cork, Ireland, sliced his drive on a 265-yard hole. The ball flew out of bounds, struck the roof of a house, ricocheted onto the green, and rolled into the cup for an unlikely ace.

2. JOHN REMINGTON

In 1959, John Remington hooked his drive on the par-3 seventh hole at the Cotsworth Golf Club in England. The 5-iron shot landed in the bunker, bounced off a drainage pipe, and hit a rake in the bunker. The ball then bounced onto the green, kissed off another ball, and rolled into the cup for a miracle hole-in-one.

3. G. C. HAZEN

Golfers are pleased when they score a birdie, delighted when they make an eagle, but G. C. Hazen was ecstatic to shoot a magpie. He hit an errant drive on the 105-yard second hole at Daylesford, Australia. The ball hit a tree, bounced off a magpie that was standing on the green, and went straight into the cup.

4. JIM HADDERER

In 1965, 16-year-old Jim Hadderer hit a shot that literally brought him to his knees. On a 190-yard hole at the Wing Park Golf Course in Elgin, Illinois, Hadderer scored a hole-in-one by hitting his drive while on his knees.

5. BILL CAREY

Bill Carey managed to lose a hole in a match with Edgar Winter at the Roehampton Golf Course in England, despite making a hole-in-one. The match took place in July 1964. It was beginning to get dark when the players reached the seventh hole. Winter's shot landed within a few feet of the cup. Carey lost sight of his drive, and figuring that the ball was lost, conceded the hole. Only later did he find his ball at the bottom of the cup.

6. DICK DOWNEY

In 1991, Dick Downey scored a hole-in-one on the sixth hole of the Oakmont Country Club in Pennsylvania. His playing partner, Les Gallagher, duplicated the feat. Gallagher, who carried a 22 handicap, won the hole because he received a stroke making his score a net 0.

7. DAVID SENIOR

On his fortieth birthday, David Senior scored a hole-in-one on the 15th hole at the Royal Lytham and St. Annes Golf Course in England. His opponent, Bill Lloyd, hit a shot that landed in the cup on the fly. The force of the landing caused both balls to bounce out of the cup. Senior's hole-in-one counted, but he lost the match by a score of 2 and 1.

8. **LARRY BRUCE**

On November 15, 1962, Larry Bruce made golf history. He decided to shorten the 480-yard fifth hole at the Hope Country Club course in Arkansas by hitting through the dog-leg. The Herculean drive flew onto the green and rolled into the cup, for the longest hole-in-one on record.

9. **MARIE ROBIE**

The longest hole-in-one by a woman was recorded by Marie Robie on September 4, 1949. She aced the 393-yard first hole of the Furnace Brook Golf Club in Wollaston, Massachusetts.

10. **R. W. BRIDGES**

In 1931, R. W. Bridges made the longest putt on record, at the Woodlawn Country Club in Kirkwood, Missouri. On a 196-yard hole he used a putter to score a hole-in-one.

Shots to Remember

R elive some of the most dramatic shots in golf history.

1. GENE SARAZEN

Gene Sarazen's double eagle at the 1935 Masters is frequently cited as the greatest shot in golf history. Sarazen trailed leader Craig Wood by three strokes when he reached the 15th hole, a par 5. Sarazen's second shot, a 4-wood, landed on the right front of the green, kicked left, and rolled into the hole for a double eagle. He had erased the three-shot deficit with one shot. Sarazen defeated Wood by five shots in a playoff to become Masters champion.

2. LARRY MIZE

On the second hole of a sudden-death playoff at the 1987 Masters, Greg Norman appeared to be in position to win his first green jacket. Norman hit his second shot onto the 11th green, while Larry Mize's approach shot ended up 45 yards to the right of the green. Mize chipped in from 140 feet for a birdie 3 to win the Masters from a stunned Greg Norman.

3. **BOB TWAY**

The 1987 Masters was not the first time Greg Norman was denied victory in a major tournament by a miraculous shot. Norman and Bob Tway were tied on the final hole at the 1986 PGA Championship, played at the Inverness Club in Toledo, Ohio. Norman was safely on the green in two, but, Tway hit his second shot in a greenside bunker. The unlucky Norman watched as Tway holed the bunker shot for a birdie and a dramatic victory.

4. **TOM WATSON**

Tom Watson was tied with Jack Nicklaus when he stepped up to the 17th tee at the 1982 U.S. Open Championship, played at the Pebble Beach Golf Links. Nicklaus was already in the clubhouse and appeared to be on his way to his fifth Open title when Watson hit his tee shot into the rough bordering the left bank of the green. Watson chipped the ball in for a birdie and went on to win the tournament by two strokes.

5. **ARNOLD PALMER**

Arnold Palmer trailed Mike Souchak by seven shots going into the final round of the 1960 U.S. Open Championship, at the Cherry Hills Country Club Course in Denver. Palmer had attempted to drive the green on the 346-yard first hole on the first three rounds and failed each time, but this time he drove the ball to within 20 feet of the hole. He two-putted for a birdie 3. Palmer birdied six of the first seven holes and shot 30 on the front nine en route to a final round of 65. Palmer's charge resulted in his first U.S. Open victory.

6. LEE TREVINO

Lee Trevino held a tenuous lead over Tony Jacklin when he got into trouble on the 17th hole in the final round of the 1972 British Open, played at Muirfield in Scotland. His lead appeared in jeopardy when his fourth shot on the par-5 hole landed off the green. Trevino chipped in for par and held on for his second British Open championship.

7. ISAO AOKI

Isao Aoki became the first Japanese player to win on the PGA Tour in dramatic fashion. On the final hole of the 1983 Hawaiian Open, he holed his approach shot for an eagle to defeat Jack Renner by one stroke.

8. BOBBY JONES

Bobby Jones hit many great shots during his illustrious career, but his greatest may have come in the 1926 British Open. Jones's mashie shot on the 71st hole of the Open, played at Royal Lytham, was so spectacular that a bronze plaque commemorates it. Jones won the tournament by two strokes.

9. TIGER WOODS

The magic of Tiger Woods was personified by a spectacular shot on the final hole of the 2000 NEC Invitational, at the Firestone Country Club in Akron, Ohio. The final round was delayed for three hours by rain. By the time Woods played the 18th hole, it was nearly dark. Tiger hit his 8-iron within two feet of the pin. Fans paid tribute to him by flicking lighters in the darkness. Woods birdied the hole to win the tournament by 11 strokes.

10. **COREY PAVIN**

Corey Pavin won his first major tournament with one of the greatest wood shots in golf history. Pavin, not known for his length with his woods, hit a masterful wood shot on the 72nd hole at the 1995 U.S. Open Championship, played at Shinnecock Hills Golf Club in Southampton, New York. It rolled within a few feet of the pin, clinching the Open title for Pavin.

Great Golfing Feats

This list pays tribute to some of golf's greatest achievements.

1. BYRON NELSON

Byron Nelson enjoyed the greatest year in PGA Tour history in 1945. That year he won 18 tournaments, including a run of 11 in a row. The winning streak lasted from March to August and ended when he finished third to amateur Freddie Haas, Jr. at the Memphis Open. During the streak, Nelson's scoring average was a brilliant 67.9 strokes per round. He earned $30,250 for his 11 straight wins. A golfer today would win more than $5 million for a similar run.

2. BOBBY JONES

No golfer has won the modern Grand Slam, which consists of the Masters, U.S. Open Championship, British Open, and PGA Championship. Before the Masters came into existence in 1934, the four tournaments recognized as the Grand Slam were the U.S. Open, U.S. Amateur, British Open, and British Amateur. The only player to win the original Grand Slam was Bobby Jones, who achieved the feat in 1930.

3. JACK NICKLAUS

Of his many career accomplishments, Jack Nicklaus's greatest was winning 18 major tournaments. Between 1962 and 1986, Nicklaus won six Masters, five PGAs, four U.S. Open Championships, and three British Opens.

4. TIGER WOODS

Twenty-four-year-old Tiger Woods became the youngest player ever to win every Grand Slam event when he won the 2000 British Open, played at the Old St. Andrews Course. In 2000, Woods duplicated Ben Hogan's feat of winning three majors in a single year. He also held scoring records for all four majors.

5. BEN HOGAN

In 1953, Ben Hogan became the first golfer to win three majors of the modern Grand Slam in the same year. Hogan won the Masters, U.S. Open Championship, and British Open. He did not compete in the PGA Championship because the dates conflicted with the British Open.

6. WALTER HAGEN

Between 1924 and 1927, Walter Hagen won four consecutive PGA championships. In those days, the tournament was in a match play format.

7. LEE TREVINO

In 1971, Lee Trevino won the national championships of three different countries over a three-week period: the U.S. Open Championship, Canadian Open, and British Open. Tiger Woods duplicated the feat in 2000, but not in successive weeks.

8. **TOM WATSON**

Tom Watson won the British Open five times, each on a different golf course. His wins came at Carnoustie (1975), Turnberry (1977), Muirfield (1980), Royal Troon (1982), and Royal Birkdale (1983).

9. **MICKEY WRIGHT**

In 1961, Mickey Wright won three majors on the LPGA Tour. Her victories came in the Titleholders Championship, U.S. Women's Open Championship, and Western Open.

10. **PETER THOMSON**

Australian Peter Thomson is the only golfer of the twentieth century to win three consecutive British Opens. He won the titles at Royal Birkdale in 1954, St. Andrews in 1955, and at Hoylake in 1956. Following a second-place finish in 1957, he won his fourth British Open at Royal Lytham in 1958. Thomson won his fifth and final British Open at Southport in 1965.

Life Begins at 60

D avid Duval made headlines in 1999 when he tied the PGA record for the lowest 18-hole score with a round of 59. All of the following golfers shot rounds of 60 or below.

1. **HOMERO BLANCAS**

Homero Blancas set the record for the lowest round in a professional tournament. On August 19, 1962, Blancas carded a 55 at the Premier Invitational Tournament in Longview, Texas. Not surprisingly, he won.

2. **ALFRED SMITH**

On January 1, 1936, Alfred Smith shot a round of 55 at a course in Woolacombe, England. The 15-under-par round bettered the existing record for a low round by two shots.

3. **LARRY NELSON**

Larry Nelson shot a 58 during the pro-am event preceding the 2000 Kroger Senior Classic in Mason, Ohio. He shot 29 on both the front and back nines. Nelson's team won the pro-am with a score of 21 under par.

4. **AL GEIBERGER**

Al Geiberger became the first golfer to break 60 in a PGA tournament when he shot 59 in the second round of the Danny Thomas Memphis Classic on June 10, 1977. The 13-under-par round came on the lengthy 7,249-yard Colonial Country Club Course. Over a seven-hole stretch, Geiberger made six birdies and an eagle. He rolled in an eight-foot birdie putt on the 18th hole to break 60. Geiberger won the tournament, his tenth career victory on the tour.

5. **CHIP BECK**

Chip Beck tied Al Geiberger's record with a 59 in the third round of the 1991 Las Vegas Invitational. Beck blistered the Sunrise Golf Club Course with 13 birdies, including six in a row. However, his round was not good enough; he finished third in the tournament behind winner Andrew Magee.

6. **MALCOLM MILLER**

In 1977, 59-year-old amateur Malcolm Miller shot his age at the Minocqua Country Club Course in Wisconsin.

7. **WANDA MORGAN**

On July 11, 1929, teenager Wanda Morgan set a women's record for the lowest 18-hole score, when she shot a 60 at the Westgate and Birchington Golf Course in Kent, England. Morgan shot 31 on the front nine and 29 on the back.

8. **AL BROSCH**

Al Brosch shot a round of 60 in the third round of the 1951 Texas Open, played at the Brackenridge Park Golf Course in San Antonio.

9. BILL NARY

Bill Nary fired a course record 60 in the third round of the 1952 El Paso Open, played at the El Paso Country Club in Texas.

10. WALLY ULRICH

In the second round of the 1954 Virginia Beach Open, played at the Cavalier Yacht and Country Club in Virginia Beach, Wally Ulrich shot a 60.

Memorable Rounds

Some rounds of golf stand out in our memory. These 10 rounds are certain to pass the test of time.

1. JOHNNY MILLER

Johnny Miller entered the final round of the 1973 U.S. Open Championship six strokes behind the leader. His final round, 63, over the difficult Oakmont Country Club Course in Pennsylvania, is considered one of the greatest rounds in golf history. Miller's historic round enabled him to win his first U.S. Open title.

2. FRANCIS OUIMET

Twenty-year-old Francis Ouimet shocked the golf world when he defeated British golfing legends Harry Vardon and Ted Ray in a three-way playoff for the 1913 U.S. Open Championship title. The tournament was played at the Country Club in Brookline, Massachusetts. Ouimet's playoff round of 72 was five shots better than Vardon and six shots ahead of Ray. Ouimet's victory helped popularize golf in the United States.

3. JACK NICKLAUS

Jack Nicklaus saved his best for last. The 46-year-old Golden Bear won his eighteenth and final major tournament at the 1986 Masters. His final round of 65 included six birdies and an eagle over the last 10 holes.

4. ARNOLD PALMER

Arnold Palmer trailed the leader Mike Souchak by seven shots going into the final round of the 1960 U.S. Open Championship, played at the Cherry Hills Country Club in Colorado. Palmer charged to a final round of 65 to win the tournament by two strokes.

5. TOM WATSON

Tom Watson and Jack Nicklaus were the greatest rivals of the 1970s, and their play in the final round at the 1977 British Open, at Turnberry, epitomized their excellence. The two men entered the final round three shots ahead of the field. Watson's final round of 65 enabled him to defeat Nicklaus by one stroke.

6. KEN VENTURI

Ken Venturi's victory at the 1964 U.S. Open Championship, played at the Congressional Country Club in Bethesda, Maryland, was one of the most dramatic in golf history. Venturi overcame heat prostration to win the tournament by four strokes over Tommy Jacobs.

7. BEN HOGAN

In 1949, Ben Hogan was involved in a near-fatal automobile accident that placed his golf career in jeopardy. A year later, at the 1950 U.S. Open Championship, played at the Merion–East course in Ardmore, Pennsylvania, he culminated his amazing comeback with a playoff win.

8. BILLY CASPER

With nine holes to play at the 1966 U.S. Open Championship, played at The Olympic Club in San Francisco, Billy Casper trailed Arnold Palmer by seven strokes. Incredibly, Casper rallied to tie Palmer after 72 holes and defeated him in an 18-hole playoff. Palmer would never win another major tournament.

9. PAUL LAWRIE

Paul Lawrie of Scotland trailed by 10 shots going into the final round of the 1999 British Open, at Carnoustie. When leader Jean Van de Velde triple-bogeyed the 72nd hole, it forced a three-way playoff with Lawrie, Van de Velde, and Justin Leonard. Lawrie won the three-hole playoff to cap the greatest comeback in British Open history.

10. ART WALL, JR.

Art Wall, Jr. began the final round of the 1959 Masters six shots behind leader Arnold Palmer. Wall birdied five of the final six holes, beating Palmer and winning his first green jacket.

Shooting for the Moon

In 1897, the Los Angeles Country Club was built on a garbage dump, and tomato cans were used as holes. Over the years, the course became an outstanding golf venue, but other courses retained their eccentricities. At the Dannebrog Golf Course in Nebraska, dozens of cows grazed on the course. The 14th hole of the Coeur d'Alene Resort Course in Idaho has a floating green that can be moved 100 yards. I think you will agree that the following are not your typical golf courses.

1. ALAN SHEPARD

Alan Shepard, America's first man in space, was a member of the 1971 *Apollo 14* crew on their moon mission. Shepard became the first golfer on the moon when he hit a 6-iron shot. Because of the reduced gravity on the lunar surface, Shepard commented that the ball went "miles and miles."

2. FLOYD ROOD

In October 1964, Floyd Rood played the longest golf course on record. He hit a ball from the Pacific coast to the Atlantic coast. Rood took 114,737 strokes and 13 months to complete his 3,397-mile journey. He lost 3,511 golf balls along the way.

3. ELEPHANT HILLS COUNTRY CLUB

Elephant Hills Country Club in Victoria Falls, Zimbabwe, was more like a wildlife reserve than a golf course. The course, built in 1975, was the home to lions, leopards, crocodiles, puff adders, and other dangerous animals. Terrified golfers were chased by elephants and charging hippos. Warthogs dug holes in the fairway and baboons stole balls from the fairways. Two years after it opened, the course was destroyed by rocket fire during a civil war in Zimbabwe.

4. BRITANNIA GOLF COURSE

Golfers in the Caribbean were suffering because of the high cost of real estate. In 1985, the Britannia Golf Course on Grand Cayman Island provided a solution. The course was only half the size of a normal 18-hole regulation course. At the Britannia's request, MacGregor, a major producer of golf equipment, manufactured a ball that traveled half as far as a regular ball. Jack Nicklaus, one of the longest hitters on the PGA Tour, demonstrated the new ball by hitting a drive that traveled 140 yards.

5. LAURENS GOLF AND COUNTRY CLUB

The Laurens Golf and Country Club in Iowa also served as an airport. A grass runway crossed seven of the course's nine fairways. Whenever a plane took off or landed, golfers ran for cover.

6. **MT. DUNDAS COUNTRY CLUB**

The Mt. Dundas Country Club in Greenland was recommended only for the hardiest golfers. Located only 800 miles from the North Pole, Mt. Dundas was a barren, rocky, 18-hole course. The "greens" were 10-foot circles of sand. Players were required to carry a carpet square from which they would hit their shots. The 18th hole may have been the toughest in golf. The green was atop a 700-foot-high hill. Golfers needed to use rock-climbing equipment to scale the 60-degree cliff.

7. **TIJUANA**

Walter Hagen and Joe Kirkwood had just finished a round at the 1928 Tijuana Open, in Mexico, when Kirkwood proposed a wager. He bet Hagen $50 that he could hit a golf ball back to their hotel first. The two professionals used the streets of Tijuana as their own personal golf course. It was decided that the toilet in their hotel room would serve as the hole. Hagen got there first but was unable to hit the ball into the toilet. Kirkwood, a noted trick shot artist, made it on his first attempt.

8. **GREEN ZONE GOLF COURSE**

The Green Zone Golf Course straddled the borders of Sweden and Finland. The sixth hole had its tee in Sweden and its green in Finland, and the green was in two separate time zones. The course also had its own customs office. Because of its proximity to the Arctic Circle, the sun never set from June through August, allowing players to golf 24 hours a day.

q. **X-RATED MINIATURE GOLF**

The Burning Man Celebration is a counterculture festival held each year in the Nevada desert. More than 25,000 people attend the celebration annually. The highlight is the torching of a 50-foot-high wooden man. Clothing is optional at the festival. An attraction of the 2000 event was an X-rated miniature golf course.

10. **HAMMERSLEY HILL GOLF AND HUNT CLUB**

Famed newscaster Lowell Thomas built his own private golf course, the Hammersley Golf and Hunt Club. Each hole featured a double green with two holes. One hole had the standard 4¼-inch cup, while the other was twice that size for less-skilled players. Presidents Dwight Eisenhower and Richard Nixon were among the famous guests who played the course.

Challenging Courses

If you think your local golf course is tough, try playing these courses.

1. PINE VALLEY

The Pine Valley Golf Club in Clementon, New Jersey, is often rated the best golf course in the United States and the most difficult golf course in the world. The layout features enormous sand traps and scrublike areas near the greens. In the late 1930s, an international tournament was played at Pine Valley featuring the greatest players in the world. The field included Sam Snead, Byron Nelson, Gene Sarazen, Craig Wood, and Horton Smith. The course was so difficult that only two of the more than 450 rounds were played under par.

2. PEBBLE BEACH

Few would argue that the Pebble Beach Golf Links is a spectacular test of golf. Situated on the Monterey Peninsula in California, Pebble Beach has hosted four U.S. Open Championships and the annual Pebble Beach Pro-Am.

Perhaps no course has more memorable holes. The seventh hole barely measures 100 yards but is a nightmare to play when it is windy. The par-4 eighth, ninth, and 10th holes are among the most challenging in golf. The closing par-5 hole requires a drive over a rocky shoreline.

3. AUGUSTA NATIONAL

Each April, the Masters Golf Tournament, the year's first major, is played at the Augusta National Golf Course in Georgia. The course's physical beauty, with its dogwoods and azaleas in bloom, belie its difficulty. The treacherous Amen Corner, the holes beginning the back nine, has destroyed the dreams of many golfers seeking their first green jacket. Rough was added to the course in 2000 to make Augusta even more difficult.

4. CYPRESS POINT CLUB

The Cypress Point Club in Pebble Beach, California, was designed by Alister Mackenzie, the architect of Augusta National. Cypress Point, overlooking the Monterey Peninsula, is one of the world's most scenic courses and among the most demanding. The 16th hole, which requires a 200-yard tee shot over water, may be the most intimidating in golf.

5. OAKMONT COUNTRY CLUB

Since 1922, the Oakmont Country Club in Pennsylvania has hosted numerous U.S. Open Championships and PGA Championships. The course is distinguished by its huge bunkers and lightning-fast greens. At one time, Oakmont had more than 220 sand traps, the most notorious being The Church Pews, a series of sand rows splitting the third and fourth fairways.

6. **WINGED FOOT-WEST**

The Winged Foot–West Course in Mamaroneck, New York, tests every aspect of a golfer's game. Winged Foot features long par-4s and small, fast greens. Bobby Jones, Billy Casper, and Hale Irwin have won U.S. Open Championships there.

7. **BALTUSROL-LOWER**

In 1903, the Baltusrol–Lower Golf Club in Springfield, New Jersey, hosted its first major tournament, the U.S. Open Championship. Jack Nicklaus won two of his Open titles at Baltusrol in 1967 and 1980. Two of its most difficult holes are the par-3 fourth, which requires a drive over a pond, and the long par-5 17th, which features a huge fairway bunker known as The Sahara.

8. **OAKLAND HILLS-SOUTH**

The Oakland Hills–South Country Club course in Birmingham, Michigan, was called a monster by Ben Hogan because of its intimidating difficulty and length. Hogan tamed the monster with a victory in the 1951 U.S. Open Championship. Tee shots frequently end up in the bunkers that line the fairways.

9. **MERION-EAST**

The Merion–East Golf Club course in Ardmore, Pennsylvania, proves that a course does not have to be extremely long to be difficult. Playing at barely 6,500 yards, Merion challenges even the most skilled golfer. Creeks run through the course, and the small, tricky greens can be a nightmare. Instead of flags, Merion has red woven baskets atop the poles marking its holes.

10. **SHINNECOCK HILLS**

The Shinnecock Hills Golf Club course in Southampton, New York, has the feel of a Scottish links course. The perils of the course include numerous bunkers, sloping fairways, and unpredictable winds.

Unholy Holes

These 10 holes brought some of the world's best golfers to their knees.

1. CYPRESS POINT—16TH HOLE

The 16th hole at Cypress Point is often referred to as the most difficult hole in golf. The 230-yard par 3 demands a tee shot over craggy rocks and ocean surf. Many a player has ended play on the rocks. Henry Ranson hit 16 shots trying to get the ball off the rocks before giving up. Groucho Marx once threw his clubs into the Pacific Ocean in frustration after failing to clear the water.

2. THE ROAD HOLE

The Road Hole, the 17th hole at St. Andrews in Scotland, has been called the most difficult par 4 in the world. David Duval dropped from second to eleventh when he quadruple-bogeyed the hole at the 2000 British Open. The long par 4 begins with a drive over the corner of the course hotel. An imposing 10-foot-deep bunker fronts the green and is nearly impossible to escape from. A road and a stone wall guard the right side of the hole. Many balls end up stymied against the wall.

3. TPC AT SAWGRASS—17TH HOLE

The 17th hole at the TPC at Sawgrass Course in Ponte Vedra, Florida, shows how difficult a 130-yard hole can be. The famed island green allows no place for a bail-out shot. Many shots that land on the green bounce into the water on the other side. Each year, more than 120,000 shots find the water, an average of two and a half shots per player.

4. THE POSTAGE STAMP

The eighth hole at Royal Troon in Scotland has been the bane of many golfers. Measuring only 126 yards, the hole's name is derived from its tiny green. The elevated green is guarded by deep bunkers. At the 1950 British Open, Herman Tissies shot a 15 on the Postage Stamp hole.

5. PINE VALLEY—SEVENTH HOLE

If Pine Valley is the most difficult golf course in the world, then the seventh may be its most intimidating hole. The long par-5 is nearly unreachable in two shots. The fairway is bisected by an enormous sand trap known as Hell's Half Acre.

6. MEDINAH—SEVENTH HOLE

Measuring nearly 600 yards, the uphill par-5 seventh hole at The Medinah Country Club Number 3 course in Illinois is almost impossible to reach in two shots. Approach shots are made difficult by a multilevel green.

7. **FIRESTONE SOUTH—16TH HOLE**

The ultimate challenge for long hitters is to reach the 625-yard 16th hole at Akron's Firestone South course in two shots. The small green of the dogleg hole is guarded by a pond in front and by pot bunkers in the back.

8. **PEBBLE BEACH—EIGHTH HOLE**

Choosing one of the most difficult holes at Pebble Beach is almost as difficult as playing them. The long par-4 eighth hole begins a stretch of three of the toughest holes in golf. The tee sits atop a cliff. The drive is blind, and if you slice the shot, your ball will likely land in Monterey Bay. The small green is surrounded by bunkers, and a scrubby bank catches errant shots.

9. **AUGUSTA—12TH HOLE**

Part of the dreaded Amen Corner at Augusta, the short par-3 12th hole always provides its share of drama at the Masters. The tee shot must clear Rae's Creek and land on a narrow green.

10. **DORAL—13TH HOLE**

The 13th hole at the Doral Blue course in Miami, Florida, has been unlucky for many golfers. The par-3 hole measures nearly 250 yards. Adding to the hole's difficulty is an elevated green guarded by bunkers.

Play for Pay

Today, purse money on the PGA, LPGA, and Senior tours is in the tens of millions of dollars, but it has not always been that way. In 1944, the entire prize money for the 22-tournament PGA Tour totaled only $150,000 and was paid out in war bonds.

1. BOBBY JONES

Bobby Jones won 13 major tournaments, including the Grand Slam in 1930. Despite winning four U.S. Open Championships and three British Opens, Jones never earned a cent for his victories because he remained an amateur throughout his career.

2. ARNOLD PALMER

Arnold Palmer won the 1955 Canadian Open for his first professional victory. Palmer did not receive a dime for his win because of an existing rule stating that a player had to be on tour for six months before he could accept prize money.

3. HOWARD TWITTY

In 2000, Tiger Woods signed a five-year deal with Nike worth an estimated $100 million. Howard Twitty's 1977 deal with Burger King was a whopper. Twitty agreed to place a Burger King logo on his golf bag in exchange for 500 Whoppers. He went on to win two tournaments and more than $2 million on the PGA Tour during his career.

4. BYRON NELSON

Byron Nelson won 52 tournaments during his career, including a record 18 in 1945. His rookie season on the tour in 1932 was less than auspicious. Nelson earned only $12.50 during his first six months as a professional.

5. JACK NICKLAUS

Jack Nicklaus won 70 tournaments in his storied career. The Golden Bear turned professional in 1962. Although he earned more than $5 million on the PGA Tour, his first professional paycheck was a measly $33.33. Later that year, Nicklaus won his first U.S. Open Championship.

6. SAM SNEAD

Sam Snead joked that he buried his prize money in tomato cans in his yard. One prospective thief even dug up his front yard in a futile attempt to find the buried treasure. When Snead won the 1937 Bing Crosby Pro-Am, he refused the $750 check from the singer, insisting that he be paid in cash. Snead earned $600 for his victory in the 1946 British Open but actually lost money since his expenses totaled $1,000.

Courtesy USGA

Bob Hope, Sam Snead, Horton Smith, and Bing Crosby
Celebrity tournaments offered fans the opportunity to see their favorite Hollywood and golf stars in the same venue. Here, Sam Snead accompanies Bing Crosby in singing a little show tune at the Bing Crosby Pro-Am.

7. JACQUELINE PUNG

When Jacqueline Pung was disqualified for signing an incorrect scorecard at the 1957 U.S. Women's Open, the $1,800 first prize was awarded to runner-up Betsy Rawls. *New York Times* writer Linc Werden passed the hat and gave the money to Pung. She received $2,500 from the collection, $700 more than she would have as the Open champion.

8. PAUL RUNYAN

Paul Runyan was the first official money winner on the PGA Tour. Runyan won seven tournaments in 1934 and earned $6,767 for the year. His expenses were $6,765, leaving him a net profit of $2.

9. MICKEY WRIGHT

Mickey Wright won 10 tournaments on the LPGA Tour in 1961. Three of her victories occurred in major tournaments. Her earnings for the year was a paltry $22,236.

10. HOWARD LUTNICK

Allison Lutnick gave her husband, Howard, a thirtieth birthday present that he will never forget. She paid $51,000 so her husband could play a round with Tiger Woods. The round took place in 2000 at the Isleworth Country Club in Windermere, Florida. Lutnick shot a respectable 93 and actually halved the 12th hole with Woods. Three other golfers paid the fee for the privilege of playing with Tiger. Ninety percent of the proceeds went to the Tiger Woods Foundation, which helps youngsters realize their dreams.

Shotguns and Daggers

Some prizes given at golf tournaments have been booby prizes. In 1932, an unidentified Kansas golfer won 35,000 pounds of crushed rock salt for his victory in a tournament.

1. BOBBY JONES

On February 22, 1930, Bobby Jones won the Savannah Open by one shot. Although he was not permitted to accept prize money, he was given a double-barreled shotgun for being the tournament's low amateur.

2. PAUL SMITH

Funeral director Paul Smith offered an unusual prize for a hole-in-one at the 1985 New South Wales Open in Canberra, Australia. Any golfer who scored an ace on the eighth hole was to be awarded a prepaid funeral by Smith, one of the tournament's sponsors. If a sudden-death playoff had occurred, it would have begun on the eighth hole.

3. IAN BAKER-FINCH

Ian Baker-Finch won the 1988 Bridgestone/Aso Open in Japan. He was astonished to learn that his prize included a cow; Aso is one of Japan's leading dairy centers. Baker-Finch sold the cow back to the tournament organizers for $5,000.

4. ABE LEMONS

Abe Lemons, basketball coach of Oklahoma City University, played in a tournament at the Frederick, Oklahoma, Golf and Country Club. Lemons popped up one of his drives, which, blown by the wind, landed 15 yards behind him. He was given a bottle of Geritol as a prize.

5. WILLIE PARK

In 1860, Willie Park won the first British Open in Prestwick, Scotland. For his victory, Park was presented with a red Moroccan leather belt.

6. LEE TREVINO

King Hassan II of Morocco sponsored his own tournament, the Moroccan Grand Prix. For winning the pro-am, Lee Trevino was presented with a bejeweled dagger.

7. GENE LITTLER

Gene Littler won the Tournament of Champions in Las Vegas for three consecutive years beginning in 1955. At the time, the prize money was awarded in silver dollars.

8. DON POOLEY

Don Pooley won a $1 million bonus for scoring a hole-in-one on the 17th hole of the 1987 Hertz Bay Hill Classic in

Orlando, Florida. The bonus exceeded the amount of prize money Pooley had won during his entire professional career.

9. JASON BOHN

Jason Bohn, a 19-year-old college student from State College, Pennsylvania, won $1 million for scoring a hole-in-one during a 1992 charity tournament in Alabama. Bohn aced the second hole at the University of Alabama Golf Course.

10. YOSHIAKA ONO

At the 1981 Singapore Open, Japanese amateur Yoshiaka Ono won a $50,000 prize for scoring a hole-in-one. Because he would have to renounce his amateur status to claim the prize, he declined it.

Discontinued Tournaments

Many tournaments of the past no longer exist. Three tournaments that had been considered majors on the LPGA Tour—the Western Open, the Titleholders Championship, and the du Maurier Classic—were discontinued. The Western Open was discontinued in 1967, the last Titleholders Championship was played in 1972, and the final du Maurier Classic took place in 2000.

1. IRON LUNG OPEN

The fifth tournament that Byron Nelson won during his record 11 consecutive tournament win streak was the now defunct Iron Lung Open in Atlanta, Georgia. Nelson set a tournament record with a 72-hole total 263.

2. BABE ZAHARIAS CANCER FUND OPEN

The Babe Zaharias Cancer Fund Open was an LPGA event during the 1950s. The tournament was named for champion golfer Babe Zaharias, who died of cancer in 1956. Betsy Rawls won the tournament in 1956.

3. THE GIRL TALK CLASSIC

During the 1970s, the Girl Talk Classic was an event on the LPGA Tour. Hall of Famer Pat Bradley won her first victory in the 1976 Girl Talk Classic.

4. DESOTO OPEN

Forty-seven-year-old Sam Snead won the 1960 DeSoto Open. The tournament was sponsored by the DeSoto automobile company. In 1961, after 33 years of manufacturing automobiles, the DeSoto automobile was discontinued, as was the golf tournament.

5. ROYAL POINCIANA INVITATIONAL

The Royal Poinciana Invitational was played at the Palm Springs Golf Club in Florida. The par-3 tournament was distinctive because it had both men and women professionals using the same tees. In 1961, Louise Suggs won the tournament.

6. LUCKY INTERNATIONAL OPEN

Ken Venturi won the 1966 Lucky International Open in his hometown of San Francisco. However, the Lucky International proved unlucky for Venturi because it was his last tournament victory.

7. RUBBER CITY OPEN

The Rubber City Open was played in Akron, Ohio. The 1957 tournament was won by Arnold Palmer, who defeated Doug Ford with a 25-foot chip shot on the sixth playoff hole.

8. **THE BETSY RAWLS PEACH BLOSSOM OPEN**

The Betsy Rawls Peach Blossom Open was named for the golfer and played in her hometown of Spartanburg, South Carolina. Rawls won her own tournament in 1956.

9. **HARDSCRABBLE OPEN**

The Hardscrabble Open was a women's tournament during the 1940s. Patty Berg was the winner in 1949.

10. **GASPARILLA OPEN**

The Gasparilla Open was a stop on the men's tour during the 1930s. The great Walter Hagen's last tournament victory occurred in the 1935 Gasparilla Open.

Women Winners

Karrie Webb had a sensational year on the LPGA Tour in 2000. Webb is just the latest in a line of great women golfers.

1. DOROTHY CAMPBELL

Dorothy Campbell was the dominant woman golfer at the turn of the twentieth century. The Scottish golfer won the amateur championships in Great Britain, the United States, and Canada. Campbell won a record 750 tournaments around the world.

2. KATHY WHITWORTH

Between 1962 and 1985, Kathy Whitworth won 88 tournaments on the LPGA Tour. Her winning total not only set a record for the LPGA Tour, but was also seven more victories than the total of the men's record holder, Sam Snead.

3. MICKEY WRIGHT

Mickey Wright was the leading women's player of the early 1960s. She won 13 tournaments on the LPGA Tour in 1963.

Before she retired in 1978, Wright won 82 tournaments and 13 majors.

4. **PATTY BERG**

Patty Berg set a women's record with 15 major tournament victories. Berg won seven Titleholders Championships, seven Western Opens, and a U.S. Open Championship title, among her 57 tour victories.

5. **BETSY RAWLS**

One of the most accomplished women golfers in history, Betsy Rawls is fourth on the all-time LPGA victory list with 55. Her best year was 1959, when she won 10 times. Eight of her victories came in major tournaments.

6. **GLENNA COLLETT VARE**

The only woman to win six U.S. Amateur Championships was Glenna Collett Vare. She won the amateur title in 1922, 1925, 1928, 1929, 1930, and 1935. The Vare Trophy, awarded annually to the player on the LPGA Tour with the lowest stroke average, was named in her honor.

7. **LOUISE SUGGS**

Louise Suggs won 50 tournaments during her career. Her 11 major tournament victories included U.S Open Championship titles in 1949 and 1952. In 1951, she was the first golfer elected into the LPGA Hall of Fame.

8. **NANCY LOPEZ**

Nancy Lopez was an instant sensation on the LPGA Tour. During her rookie season in 1978, she won nine tournaments, including a record five in a row. Lopez won eight

tournaments the next year and has more than 45 victories
on the LPGA Tour.

9. **SANDRA HAYNIE**

Sandra Haynie won 42 tournaments on the LPGA Tour. She
led the tour in victories in 1974 and 1975.

10. **CAROL MANN**

Carol Mann won 38 LPGA tournaments. Her best year was
1968, in which she won 10 tournaments. The next year, she
led the tour with eight victories.

Men Winners

Tiger Woods already has more than 20 victories on the PGA Tour. All of the following golfers have more than 35 victories.

1. SAM SNEAD

Sam Snead holds a number of records on the PGA Tour. Between 1936 and 1965, Snead won a record 81 tournaments. His victories included three Masters and three PGA Championships.

2. JACK NICKLAUS

Second on the all-time tournament victory list with 70, Jack Nicklaus was the PGA Player of the Year five times between 1967 and 1976.

3. BEN HOGAN

Despite being involved in a near-fatal automobile accident in 1949, Ben Hogan won 63 tournaments on the PGA Tour. He did not win his first tournament until he was 28 years old, nine years after he first joined the Tour in 1931.

4. **ARNOLD PALMER**

The most charismatic golfer of his time, Arnold Palmer won 60 tournaments on the PGA Tour and another 19 abroad. His eight major titles included four Masters championships.

5. **BYRON NELSON**

Despite retiring at age 34, Byron Nelson won 52 tournaments. His 18 tournament victories in 1945 are more than most golfers win in a career.

6. **BILLY CASPER**

Billy Casper won the Vardon Trophy five times during the 1960s. Overshadowed by Arnold Palmer and Jack Nicklaus, Casper won an impressive 51 times on the tour.

7. **WALTER HAGEN**

Golf's first great showman, Walter Hagen won 40 tournaments during his career. His 11 major professional titles rank second to Jack Nicklaus.

8. **CARY MIDDLECOFF**

Cary Middlecoff did not turn professional until 1947, when he was 26 years old. Despite such a late start and back problems that forced an early retirement, Middlecoff won 40 tournaments on the PGA Tour.

9. **GENE SARAZEN**

Gene Sarazen is one of only five golfers to have won all four major tournaments. Sarazen's 38 tour victories included seven major titles.

10. **LLOYD MANGRUM**

One of the unsung golfers of his time, Lloyd Mangrum's 36 tour victories rank him ahead of such greats as Tom Watson, Lee Trevino, and Gary Player. His only major victory occurred in the 1946 U.S. Open Championship.

Runaway Winners

P aul Runyan won the 1938 PGA with an 8 and 7 victory in the championship match against Sam Snead. "Long" Jim Barnes, who sucked on sprigs of clover and grass while he played, won the 1921 U.S. Open Championship by nine strokes. Patty Sheehan set a tournament record for margin of victory when she won the 1984 LPGA Championship by 10 shots. All of the following players won tournaments or matches by double-digit figures.

1. BOBBY JONES

Bobby Jones and Al Espinosa finished the 1929 U.S. Open Championship, played at the Winged Foot Golf Course in Mamaroneck, New York, tied for the lead with a 72-hole score of 294. A 36-hole playoff was arranged to determine the winner. Jones routed Espinosa by an incredible 23 shots, 141 to 164.

2. JERRY PATE

In 1982, Jerry Pate set a record for the largest winning margin in a professional tournament when he won the Colombian Open by 21 strokes.

3. **ARCHIE COMPSTON**

British professional Archie Compston played an exhibition match against Walter Hagen at the Moor Park golf course in London in 1928. Hagen, one of the greatest match play golfers of all time, had just won four consecutive PGA Championships. Compston shocked Hagen by trouncing him 18 and 17. Undaunted by the humiliating defeat, Hagen won the British Open the following week by three strokes over Compston.

4. **RALPH GULDAHL**

In 1928, Byron Nelson and Ralph Guldahl played a 72-hole caddie match at the Bob-O-Link Golf Club in Dallas. Both golfers were 16 years old at the time. After 54 holes, Guldahl held an 18-hole lead with 18 holes to play, so it was not necessary to play the final round. Guldahl and Nelson went on to brilliant professional careers. Guldahl won the U.S. Open Championship in 1937 and 1938, and Nelson won the Open the next year.

5. **CECILIA LEITCH**

Cecilia Leitch set a women's record for the largest victory margin in match play at the 1921 Canadian Ladies Open Championship at Rivermend, Ottawa, Canada. She won the championship match 17 and 15.

6. **DOUGLAS EDGAR**

Douglas Edgar broke the tournament record by 17 strokes when he shot 278 at the 1919 Canadian Open. His winning margin was 16 strokes ahead of runner-up Bobby Jones.

7. BOBBY LOCKE

Bobby Locke demolished the field at the 1948 Chicago Victory National Championship played at the Midlothian Country Club. The South African won the championship by 16 strokes.

Bobby Locke   Courtesy USGA

South African golfer Bobby Locke, one of the greatest putters in golf history, earned the nickname "Muffin Face."

8. TIGER WOODS

Tiger Woods dominated golf in the year 2000. He won three major championships: the U.S. Open Championship, British Open, and PGA Championship. Nowhere was his superiority more evident than at the 2000 U.S. Open, played at Pebble Beach Golf Course. Woods distanced the field by 15 shots. Three years earlier, Woods won the Masters by 12 shots.

9. LOUISE SUGGS

Louise Suggs easily won the 1949 U.S. Women's Open Championship, played at the Prince Georges Golf Course in Landover, Maryland. She finished the event 14 strokes in front of the second-place finisher, Babe Zaharias.

10. BABE ZAHARIAS

It appeared that Babe Zaharias's golf career was over when she was diagnosed with cancer in 1953. She capped off an amazing comeback by winning the 1954 U.S. Women's Open Championship, played at the Salem Country Club in Peabody, Massachusetts, by a dozen strokes.

Marathon Golf

Some players cannot get enough golf. In 1983, Irvin Hemmle of Fort Worth, Texas, hit 48,265 practice shots. Welsh golfer David Morris hit 1,290 practice drives, an average of one every three seconds, during a session in 1988. Charles Stock of Lyndhurst, Ohio, played 44 rounds of golf at the Arcadia Country Club course on July 20, 1987. Colin Young played 70 rounds at the Patshull Park Golf Club in Pattingham, England, during a week in July 1989.

1. JACK NICKLAUS

In January 1991, Jack Nicklaus played 18 holes on 18 different golf courses in the Palm Beach, Florida, area. Transported by helicopter, Nicklaus shot a par 73 for the unusual round, which took less than nine hours to play. The exhibition was staged to raise money for a local charity.

2. SIMON CLOUGH AND BORIS JANJIC

Englishman Simon Clough and Australian Boris Janjic played rounds of golf in five different European countries in one day in 1992. The two golfers played in France, Luxembourg,

Germany, Holland, and Belgium. Despite the excessive travel, they averaged a respectable 77 shots per round.

3. ERNEST SMITH

Ernest Smith played rounds of golf in five different countries on June 12, 1939. Smith played rounds in Scotland, Ireland, the Isle of Man, England, and Wales. His scores for the day were 70, 76, 76, 72, and 68.

4. ALAIN REISCO

Alain Reisco, an airline executive, played rounds of golf on three different continents in one day. His playing partners for the transcontinental match were Sherl Folger, Marvin Fritz, and Art Sues. At dawn, the foursome teed off at the Royal Mohammedia course in Morocco. They played an afternoon round at the Torrequebrada Golf Course in Malaga, Spain. By early evening, they were playing the North Hills Country Club in Manhasset, New York.

5. RALPH KENNEDY

Between 1910 and 1953, Ralph Kennedy played rounds on 3,615 different golf courses. He played on courses in all 50 states and in 13 foreign countries.

6. JACK REDMOND

Jack Redmond, an American businessman, played golf at more than 2,800 courses around the world. He played in 41 different countries, primarily during the 1950s.

7. GEORGE NEW

In 1922, George New and W. R. Chamberlain began a match that ended up lasting a lifetime. New and Chamberlain played a round every Thursday at the Littlecote Golf Club in England. The two men played once a week until New's death in 1938. New won the match by 1,637 strokes, 42,371 to 44,008.

8. **BILLY BURKE**

Billy Burke was tied with George Von Elm after 72 holes at the 1931 U.S. Open Championship. The tournament was played at the Inverness Country Club in Toledo, Ohio. Still tied after a 36-hole playoff, Burke prevailed by one shot after 72 playoff holes.

9. **DAVID CAVALIER**

Using a golf cart, David Cavalier played 846 holes of golf on August 6, 1990, at the Arrowhead Country Club in North Canton, Ohio. This remarkable feat was the equivalent of 47 rounds in one day.

10. **OLLIE BOWERSOF**

Ollie Bowersof of Gaffney, South Carolina, played 10,075 holes of golf in one year. He averaged more than a round and a half of golf each day.

Weather Not Fit for Golfers nor Beasts

G olf is a game at the mercy of the weather. Adverse conditions include rain, lightning, hail, and high winds.

1. LEE TREVINO, JERRY HEARD, BOBBY NICHOLS

Lee Trevino, Jerry Heard, and Bobby Nichols were injured by lightning during the second round of the 1975 Western Open, played at the Butler National Golf Club, near Chicago. The three players were huddled next to the 13th green when lightning struck nearby. Trevino, who was leaning against his golf bag, was lifted a foot in the air and fell to the ground. His back was burned. Heard, also thrown to the ground, was temporarily unable to open his hands. He suffered from burns to his groin. Nichols, who was holding an 8-iron and had a steel plate in his head, was knocked for a somersault by the force of the lightning strike. All three golfers were hospitalized. Trevino and Nichols withdrew from the tournament. Heard miraculously managed to complete the tournament and finished third. It took Trevino, one of the best golfers of his time, months to regain his form. Neither Nichols, the 1964 PGA champion, nor Heard, one of the most promising players on the tour, ever played as well again.

2. **LARRY LUJACK**

Larry Lujack did not let cold weather stop him from playing a round of golf at the Buffalo Grove Golf Club in Illinois, in January 1985. Despite a temperature of nearly 30 degrees below zero and a wind chill at 75 below zero, Lujack shot a round in the 90s.

3. **ROGER MALTBIE**

Golfers were forced to play in frigid conditions during the second round of the 1979 Memorial Tournament, played at the Muirfield Village Golf Course in Dublin, Ohio. Players endured wind chills as low as 13 degrees. As a result, 42 players failed to break 80. Roger Maltbie, the 1976 champion, shot a 92.

4. **MRS. JACK NICKLAUS**

Over the years, the Memorial Tournament has been plagued by bad weather. In 1993, rain interrupted the tournament for the fourth consecutive year. The Muirfield Village course was built on a nineteenth-century cemetery. Hoping to placate the golfing gods, Mrs. Jack Nicklaus, wife of the tournament's host, placed glasses of gin on the grounds. The rains stopped and Paul Azinger went on to win the tournament.

5. **MARY BROWN**

Rain halted play during the Southern California Women's Open. The sudden downpour left the greens flooded. Mary Brown attempted to putt out on the 18th green. The cup was still filled with water, and her putt floated right over the hole.

The water was removed from the cup and Brown was given a second chance. She promptly drained the putt.

6. **MORTON SHAPIRO**

Thanks to an act of nature, Morton Shapiro scored a hole-in-one in 1956 on the fifth hole of the Indian Springs Country Club in Marlton, New Jersey. His tee shot rolled to the lip of the cup. As he walked to the green, Shapiro felt the ground shake. An earth tremor caused his ball to fall into the cup for a hole-in-one.

7. **CHUCK ROTAR**

Chuck Rotar was not as lucky as Morton Shapiro when an earthquake occurred while he was playing in the 1962 Orange County Open in California. Rotar hit his approach shot onto the edge of the green. As he walked toward the ball, an earthquake shook the course. Rotar's ball rolled into a greenside lake. The shaken golfer, who expected to be putting for birdie, instead carded a double bogey.

8. **JOHNNY WEISSMULLER**

Johnny Weissmuller won three Olympic gold medals and was considered the greatest swimmer of his time. Weissmuller played in the 1952 Bing Crosby Pro-Am in California. The tournament was played in a drenching rain, prompting the fabled swimmer to remark, "I've never been so wet in my life."

9. **REG WHITCOMBE**

The final round of the 1938 British Open, played at the Royal St. George's Golf Club in Sandwich, England, was played in tremendously windy conditions. The winds were strong enough to blow over the exhibition tent. Reg Whitcombe won the tournament, despite shooting a final round of 78.

10. GEORGE BUSH

Former president George Bush traveled to Bermuda for a conference with British Prime Minister Margaret Thatcher. He was scheduled to play a round of golf with Thatcher's husband, Denis. Despite heavy rain and high winds, Bush insisted on finishing his round.

Water Hazards

Water can be a golfer's worst enemy.

1. MRS. J. F. MEEHAN

Mrs. J. F. Meehan was a firm believer in the motto, "Play the ball where it lies." She was playing at the 1913 Shawnee Invitational For Ladies at Shawnee-on-Delaware, Pennsylvania, when she hit an errant tee shot on the par-3 16th hole. The ball landed in the Binniekill River and began floating downstream. Rather than taking a penalty shot and rehitting her drive, Mrs. Meehan insisted on chasing after the ball. She got into a boat and rowed a mile and a half downstream. Once she reached the ball, it took her 40 shots to hit it onto land. Once on dry ground, she hacked the ball through the dense forest until she finally reached the green. By the time her score was tallied, she had taken 161 strokes to complete the 126-yard hole.

2. ANGELO SPAGNOLA

In 1985, *Golf Digest* sponsored a tournament to determine the worst avid golfer in the United States. The winner (or loser depending on your point of view) was Angelo Spagnola of Fayette City, Pennsylvania. Spagnola needed 257 strokes to complete the 18 holes, 49 more than runner-up Jack Pulford. On the 17th hole, a 138-yard par 3 that plays over a water hazard, Spagnola shot 66, a score higher than some pros shoot for 18 holes. Spagnola hit 27 balls into the water. His foursome hit 102 balls into the water that day. They also amassed 124 penalty strokes and missed the ball entirely 17 times.

3. T. J. MOORE

At the 1978 Dryden Invitational, played at the Port Arthur Country Club course in Texas, T. J. Moore hit 20 consecutive shots into the water on the 18th hole. After the penalty shots were added in, Moore needed 45 shots to complete the hole.

4. EDITH BOLLING WILSON

Edith Bolling Wilson, wife of President Woodrow Wilson, was an avid, if not very skilled, golfer. Once on a par-4 hole at a course in Hot Springs, Arkansas, the first lady topped her drive into a mud puddle. It took Mrs. Wilson, who was playing in a long skirt, 17 shots to get the ball out of the puddle.

5. BRUCE DEVLIN

Bruce Devlin's exercise in futility at the 1975 Andy Williams San Diego Open is commemorated by a plaque at the Torrey Pines Golf Course. Devlin came to the final hole two shots behind the leader. Needing an eagle to tie, he hit his second shot into a water hazard. As the horrified crowd watched, Devlin took seven shots to hit the ball out of the water. On this one hole, he had slipped from third place to thirtieth.

6. **RAY AINSLEY**

On June 10, 1938, Ray Ainsley experienced one of the worst holes in major championship history at the U.S. Open Championship, played at the Cherry Hills Country Club in Englewood, Colorado. Ainsley hit his ball into a creek and took 13 shots to get it out, finishing the hole 12 over par. He shot 96 for the round, 20 strokes more than his previous round.

7. **JOHN DALY**

John Daly, winner of two major tournaments, had a hole he would rather forget at the 1988 Bay Hill Invitational in Orlando, Florida. Daly hit six shots into the water on the par-5 sixth hole. His final tally—a 13-over-par 18.

8. **TOM WEISKOPF**

The 12th hole at Augusta National proved to be the undoing of Tom Weiskopf at the 1980 Masters. Weiskopf hit five consecutive tee shots into Rae's Creek on the short par 3. By the time the damage was done, Weiskopf took 13 strokes on the hole.

9. **PORKY OLIVER**

Porky Oliver, runner-up at the 1953 Masters, was one of the many golfers who fell victim to the treacherous 16th hole at Cypress Point in Pebble Beach, California. While competing in the 1954 Bing Crosby Pro-Am, Oliver hit four shots into the ocean and shot 16 on the par-3 hole.

10. TOMMY NAKAJIMA

At the 1978 Masters, the 13th hole at Augusta National Golf Course proved to be unlucky for Tommy Nakajima. He was assessed five penalty shots on the hole after hitting his ball into Rae's Creek. His woes included grounding the club and having the ball strike his foot. Nakajima required 13 shots to complete the par-5 hole.

Exercises in Futility

At the 1985 tournament to determine the worst avid golfer in America, Kelly Ireland met his match on the 529-yard 11th hole. He used every club in his bag and took 24 shots before he put a ball in the fairway. Ireland lived up to his reputation as one of the nation's worst golfers by shooting 179 for the round. What makes this even more astonishing is that his score was best in his foursome. This list is dedicated to all of golf's duffers.

1. CHEVALIER VON CITTERN

In 1888, Chevalier von Cittern played the worst round in golf history on a course in Biarritz, France. He averaged nearly 18 shots per hole, during his round of 316.

2. A. J. LEWIS

The worst putting performance in golf history belongs to A. J. Lewis. In 1890, he putted the ball 156 times on one hole at a course in Peacehaven, Sussex, England. Unable to make the putt, he picked up his ball and went on to the next hole.

3. FIDEL CASTRO

During the early 1960s, Fidel Castro heard of President John F. Kennedy's skill as a golfer. It was at the height of the Cold War, and the Cuban premier wanted to prove that he was a better golfer than the American president. Since a head-to-head match was out of the question, Castro decided to display his golfing prowess on the Colinas de Villareal course near Havana. He and fellow revolutionary Ché Guevara played while dressed in military uniforms. Guevara shot 127 while Castro's score exceeded 150, nearly twice the average round of Kennedy.

4. TOMMY ARMOUR

Even the best golfers can have an off day. Tommy Armour won the United States Open, British Open, and PGA championships during his career. At the 1927 Shawnee Open, Armour hit 10 shots out of bounds and shot 22 on a single hole.

5. PHILIPPE PORQUIER

No matter how hard he tried, Philippe Porquier could not hit the ball on the green at the 13th hole at the La Baule Golf Course during the 1978 French Open. Porquier shanked shot after shot out of bounds on the par-5 hole. Finally, he aimed away from the green and shanked it right onto the putting surface. Porquier's 20 was the worst single-hole score in the history of the European Tour.

6. HANS MERRELL

Hans Merrell found out why the 16th hole at Cypress Point in Pebble Beach, California, has the reputation of being one of the most difficult holes in the world. He shot a 19 on the par-3 hole at the 1959 Bing Crosby Pro-Am. After driving just short of the green, Merrell was unable to hit the ball out of an ice plant, a thorny type of vegetation, that guarded the green. Only after he teed off again was he able to finish the hole.

7. **WILLIE CHISHOLM**

Scotsman Willie Chisholm shot 18 on the par-3 eighth hole at the 1919 U.S. Open Championship, played at the Brae Burn Country Club in West Newton, Massachusetts. His tee shot on the 185-yard hole lodged against a boulder, short of the green. Finding himself between a rock and a hard place, Chisholm took 13 swings before he could unlodge the ball.

8. **NEIL COLES**

After the qualifying round for the News of the World Match-play Championship at Dunstable Downs Golf Course, Neil Coles was not feeling very chipper. On the 126-yard par-3, Coles fired his tee shot into a greenside bunker. He repeatedly tried to chip the ball out of the steep-faced bunker, without success. Finally, he chipped backward onto the fairway. Coles's misadventure in the bunker resulted in a 16 on the hole.

9. **HERMANN TISSIES**

The eighth hole at the Royal Troon Golf Course in Scotland is known as the Postage Stamp because of its tiny green. German amateur Hermann Tissies discovered just how difficult it is to hit that green. He hit a total of nine bunker shots from the three bunkers surrounding the hole. Tissies then three-putted the hole for a 15.

10. **GREG NORMAN**

Greg Norman's worst hole as a professional came at the 1982 Martini International at Lindrick. On a par-4 hole, he was distracted on his backswing by the flash of a photographer's camera. Norman hit the ball into the bushes and took a 14 on the hole.

Eighty Is Enough

The following players shot rounds of 80 or higher and still won major tournaments, set a course record, and won Olympic gold.

1. **MARGARET ABBOTT**

For the first and only time, women's golf was an Olympic event at the 1900 Paris Olympics. Ten women, from the United States and France, entered the event. One of the competitors was Margaret Abbott, a 22-year-old art student from Chicago. Abbott did not even know that she was taking part in an Olympic event. At the time, she believed she was competing in the French Amateur Championship. Abbott led an American sweep of the medals. The French competitors were hampered because they insisted on playing in tight skirts and high heels. Abbott's winning score for the nine-hole competition was an unremarkable 47. Her mother, novelist Mary Abbott, tied for seventh place, shooting a 65.

2. **JAMES DURHAM**

In 1767, James Durham set a course record when he shot a round of 94 at St. Andrews Golf Links in Scotland. The course record stood 86 years, until it was broken by John Campbell Stewart, who shot a 90 at the 1853 King William IV Gold Medal Tournament.

3. LOUIS JAMES

Nineteen-year-old Louis James shot a 94 in the qualifying round for the 1902 U.S. Amateur Championship, played at the Glen View Golf Club near Chicago. James's score was the highest of 64 golfers who moved on into the match play format. Despite the shaky opening round, James advanced through the tournament and defeated Eben Byers 4 and 2 to win the title.

4. TOM KIDD

Tom Kidd won a major golf tournament averaging 90 strokes per round. He won the 1873 British Open, played at St. Andrews, with a 36 hole total of 179.

5. BOB MARTIN

Bob Martin and David Strath were tied for the lead after 36 holes at the 1876 British Open, played at St. Andrews. Their score of 176 was an average of 88 strokes per round. Martin was declared the winner when Strath refused to compete in a playoff.

6. WILLIE PARK

Willie Park won the inaugural British Open in 1860. Three 12-hole rounds were played at the Prestwick Golf Club in Scotland, with the tournament lasting only one day. Park's winning score of 174 averaged 87 shots for every 18 holes.

7. **WILLIE ANDERSON**

Willie Anderson and Alex Smith were tied for the lead after 71 holes at the 1901 U.S. Open Championship, played at the Myopia Hunt Club in Boston. Anderson shot an 85 to win the 18-hole playoff by one shot.

8. **CHARLES SANDS**

American Charles Sands won the Olympic gold medal in golf at the 1900 Paris Olympics. His 36-hole score of 167 was good for a one-stroke victory.

9. **JOHN TAYLOR**

John Taylor's first British Open victory came at the 1894 tournament, played at Royal St. George's in England. His score of 326 was the highest winning 72-hole total in the history of the event. Taylor won the Open four more times. His winning total of 295 at the 1909 British Open, played at the Deal Course, was 31 shots better than his 1894 winning tally.

10. **GEORGE DUNCAN**

Today, any golfer opening with two rounds in the 80s would not make the cut. In 1920, George Duncan shot 80 in both his first and second rounds at the Deal Golf Course, yet still won the British Open by two strokes.

No Lead Is Safe

These players found out the hard way that no lead is too large in a golf tournament.

1. AL WATROUS

Al Watrous seemed a certain winner when he opened up a nine-shot lead with 12 holes to play at the 1932 PGA Championship, played at the Keller Golf Course in St. Paul, Minnesota. Bobby Cruickshank shot a 30 on the back nine to tie Watrous and defeated him in a playoff.

2. TOMMY BOLT

Tommy Bolt appeared on his way to victory when he fired rounds of 64 and 62 at the 1954 Virginia Beach Open, played at the Cavalier Country Club. Bolt's seven-stroke lead was down to one entering the final hole. Bolt hit a shot into the water and double-bogeyed, allowing Pete Cooper to win the tournament.

3. GREG NORMAN

Greg Norman began the final round of the 1996 Masters five strokes ahead of Nick Faldo. The Australian's quest for his first green jacket was thwarted when he shot a 6-over-par 78. Faldo's final round of 67 was good for a five-shot victory.

4. CURTIS STRANGE

At the 1985 Masters, Curtis Strange had a four-stroke lead with nine holes to play. Strange hit balls into the water on both the 13th and 15th holes, opening the door for the eventual winner, Bernhard Langer. Strange finished in a tie for second with Raymond Floyd and Seve Ballesteros.

5. T. C. CHEN

T. C. Chen of Taiwan led the 1985 U.S. Open Championship, played at Oakland Hills in Michigan, by four shots when he came to the fifth hole in the final round. Chen quadruple-bogeyed the hole after double-hitting a chip shot. The disastrous hole proved costly—Chen finished one shot behind winner Andy North.

6. KEN VENTURI

Beginning the final round, Ken Venturi led the 1956 Masters by four shots; he then bogeyed six holes on the back nine en route to a final round of 80. Jackie Burke came from eight shots behind to win the Masters.

7. MARTY FLECKMAN

Little-known Marty Fleckman led the 1967 U.S. Open Championship, played at Beltusrol in New Jersey, after three rounds. Fleckman, winner of only one PGA Tour event, ballooned to an 80, dropping to eighteenth place. Jack Nicklaus fired a final round of 65 to win by four strokes over Arnold Palmer.

8. PATTY SHEEHAN

Patty Sheehan enjoyed a nine-shot lead at the halfway point of the 1990 U.S. Women's Open Championship, played at the Salem Country Club in Massachusetts. Sheehan shot 8 over par for the last 27 holes and finished one stroke behind winner Betsy King.

9. GIL MORGAN

Gil Morgan became the first golfer ever to reach 10 under par in a U.S. Open Championship at the 1992 Open, played at Pebble Beach. During the third round, Morgan was 12 under par and opened up a commanding seven-shot lead. On the final day, Morgan shot 81 and finished thirteenth. Tom Kite was one of the few players able to master the windy conditions and won the tournament.

10. BILLY JOE PATTON

Halfway through the final round of the 1954 Masters, amateur Billy Joe Patton charged to the lead with a 32 on the front nine. His improbable victory was denied when he hit his approach shot into the water on the par-5 13th hole. Patton also bogeyed the 15th and finished one stroke behind winner Sam Snead.

Classic Collapses

All of these golfers had victories within their grasp only to let it slip away on the final few holes.

1. MATT GOGEL

Tiger Woods staged one of his most incredible comebacks at the 2000 AT&T Pebble Beach National Pro-Am. Matt Gogel blew a seven-shot lead with seven holes to play, as Woods charged to victory.

2. ARNOLD PALMER

Known for his charges, Arnold Palmer experienced one of golf's most humiliating collapses at the 1966 U.S. Open Championship, played at the Olympic Golf Club in San Francisco. Palmer led Billy Casper by seven shots with nine holes to play, but a 39 on the back nine was his undoing. The two men finished tied for the lead, but Casper won the playoff.

3. FRANKLIN LANGHAM

Franklin Langham led Jim Furyk by six shots with seven holes to play at the 2000 Doral Open in Florida. Furyk's 30 on the back nine carried him to victory.

4. DAVID AYTON

David Ayton was two holes away from victory at the 1885 British Open. He carried a five-stroke lead to the notorious Road Hole at St. Andrews. Ayton took an 11 on the hole and finished two shots behind winner Bob Martin.

5. SAM SNEAD

The United States Open was the only major championship that Sam Snead did not win. His most heartbreaking defeat occurred in the 1939 Open, played at the Spring Mill Course in Philadelphia. Snead bogeyed the 17th hole and triple-bogeyed 18 to finish a shot behind winner Byron Nelson.

6. JEAN VAN DE VELDE

Frenchman Jean Van de Velde led by three shots when he teed off at the 487-yard 18th hole during the final round of the 1999 British Open, at Carnoustie, Scotland. Van de Velde hit shots in the rough, the Barry Burn water hazard, and a greenside bunker for a triple-bogey 7. Stunned, he lost a playoff to Paul Lawrie. Months later, Van de Velde played the hole using only a putter and scored a 6.

7. MIKE REID

Mike Reid was three shots ahead with three holes to play at the 1989 PGA Championship, played at Kemper Lakes Golf Course in Long Grove, Illinois. Reid bogeyed the 16th hole, then triple-bogeyed 17 when he three-putted from four feet. Payne Stewart passed Reid to become the 1989 PGA champion.

8. CHARLES COODY

Charles Coody led the 1970 Masters with three holes to play, but he bogeyed the final three holes to finish fifth. Billy Casper won the tournament. The next year, Coody won the Masters by two strokes over Jack Nicklaus and Johnny Miller.

9. ED SNEED

Ed Sneed bogeyed the final three holes at the 1979 Masters, forcing a three-way playoff with Fuzzy Zoeller and Tom Watson. Zoeller prevailed and Sneed lost his best chance for a major title.

10. LEE TREVINO

Lee Trevino lost a three-shot lead at the 1970 British Open, played at St. Andrews, because of a mental error. He hit an approach shot to the wrong flagstick on one of St. Andrews's double greens, and the mistake precipitated his demise. Jack Nicklaus took advantage of Trevino's collapse and went on to victory. Trevino rebounded to win the British Open the next two years.

The Tournament of Their Lives

None of these players ever won a major tournament, but for one week they played record-breaking golf.

1. MIKE SOUCHAK

Mike Souchak set a PGA Tour record for the lowest 72-hole total at the 1955 Texas Open, played at the Brackenridge Golf Club in San Antonio. Souchak shot rounds of 60, 68, 64, and 65 for a 27-under-par total of 257.

2. ANDREW MAGEE

Andrew Magee established the 90-hole PGA Tour scoring record at the 1991 Las Vegas Invitational. Magee fired rounds of 69, 65, 67, 62, and 66, for a 31-under-par score of 329.

3. D. A. WEIBRING

Andrew Magee won the 1991 Las Vegas Invitational in a playoff with D. A. Weibring. Weibring's scores for the tournament were 70, 64, 65, 64, and 66.

4. LEONARD TUPLING

Leonard Tupling won the 1981 Nigerian Open, played at the Ikoyi Golf Club Course in Lagos. The British golfer shot rounds of 63, 66, 62, and 64, for a record-breaking 29-under-par 255.

5. DONNIE HAMMOND

Donnie Hammond played remarkably consistent golf to win the 1989 Texas Open, played at the Oak Hills Country Club in San Antonio. Hammond shot rounds of 65, 64, 65, and 64, for a 72-hole score of 258.

6. CHANDLER HARPER

Chandler Harper blistered the Brackenridge Park Golf Course at the 1954 Texas Open. After shooting a 70 in the first round, Harper shot 63 in the final three rounds, for a winning score of 259.

7. TIM NORRIS

Tim Norris won the 1982 Sammy Davis, Jr. Greater Hartford Open, played at the Wethersfield Country Club. Norris finished the tournament with a 25-under-par total of 259.

8. ROBERT WRENN

Robert Wrenn set a tournament record when he won the 1987 Buick Open, played at the Warwick Hills Golf and Country Club in Grand Blanc, Michigan. His 26-under-par 262 was six shots better than the record set by Ken Green in 1985.

9. **CHIP BECK**

Chip Beck is remembered for his round of 59 at the 1991 Las Vegas Invitational, but he also shot low scores during a record-breaking week at the 1988 USF&G Classic in New Orleans. Beck won the tournament with a 26-under-par score of 262.

10. **JOHN HUSTON**

John Huston burned up the course during the 1992 Walt Disney/Oldsmobile Classic in Lake Buena Vista, Florida. Huston's 26-under-par total included a 62 in the final round.

Unlikely Major Champions

The Masters, U.S. Open Championship, British Open, and PGA Championship are golf's four major tournaments. The major tournaments are usually associated with the names of great champions, such as Jack Nicklaus, Bobby Jones, Walter Hagen, and Tiger Woods. Occasionally, a golfer with less impressive credentials wins a major.

1. JOHN DALY

John Daly was the ninth alternate at the 1991 PGA Championship played at the Crooked Stick Golf Club in Carmel, Indiana. On the eve of the tournament, eight golfers withdrew, allowing Daly to become a last-minute entrant. Daly made the most of his unexpected opportunity. The 25-year-old tour rookie averaged more than 300 yards per drive and won his first major championship by three strokes over runner-up Bruce Lietzke.

2. JACK FLECK

Jack Fleck was an overwhelming underdog when he matched in a playoff with Ben Hogan for the 1955 U.S. Open

Championship, at the Olympic Country Club in San Francisco. Fleck, a municipal golf professional from Iowa, had never won a tournament, whereas Hogan was recognized as one of golf's all-time greats. Fleck pulled off one of the greatest upsets when he defeated Hogan in the playoff by three shots.

3. BOB HAMILTON

The championship match of the 1944 PGA Championship featured Byron Nelson and Bob Hamilton. Nelson, the tour's leading money winner, was a 1 to 10 favorite to defeat Hamilton, an obscure professional from Indiana who was playing in his first PGA Championship. Hamilton upset Nelson 1 up to win the tournament, played at the Manito Golf and Country Club in Spokane, Washington.

4. ORVILLE MOODY

In 1968, Orville Moody joined the PGA Tour after a 14-year stint in the U.S. Army. Moody was not considered a contender at the 1969 United States Open Championship, played at the Champions' Golf Club in Houston, Texas. Moody overcame his inconsistent putting to win the Open for his only career victory on the PGA Tour.

5. JEFF SLUMAN

Jeff Sluman won his first tour victory at the 1988 PGA championship, played at the Oaktree Golf Club in Edmond, Oklahoma. He shot a final round of 65 for a three-stroke victory.

6. JERRY PATE

Tour rookie Jerry Pate won the 1976 U.S. Open Championship, played at the Atlanta Athletic Club course. Pate birdied the final hole for his first tour win.

7. **SAM PARKS, JR.**

The only tournament victory Sam Parks, Jr. had before he played in the 1935 U.S. Open Championship was in the Western Pennsylvania Junior Championship. Parks, who was a member of the Oakmont Country Club, won the U.S. Open on his home course.

8. **WAYNE GRADY**

Australian Wayne Grady was a surprise winner at the 1990 PGA Championship, played at the Shoal Creek Country Club in Birmingham, Alabama. Grady's only previous tour victory came in the 1989 Westchester Classic.

9. **FRED MCLEOD**

Fred McLeod seemed an unlikely candidate to be the 1908 U.S. Open Championship winner. He weighed barely 100 pounds and carried only seven clubs in his bag. McLeod overcame the odds by winning the Open, played at the Myopia Hunt Club in Massachusetts.

10. **FRANCIS OUIMET**

Twenty-year-old Francis Ouimet's chance of winning the 1913 U.S. Open Championship looked slim. Although the tournament was played at the Country Club in Brookline, Massachusetts, where Ouimet had learned the game as a caddie, he seemed overmatched by veteran players such as Harry Vardon and Ted Ray. The unheralded young American defeated the Englishmen in a playoff to become the Open champion. Ouimet's caddie for the tournament was a 10-year-old boy.

Best Player Never to Have Won a Major

The label no player wants is "Best Player Never to Have Won a Major." In the past decade, players such as Paul Azinger, Tom Kite, Davis Love III, and Mark O'Meara finally won major tournaments, shedding their stigmas.

1. HARRY COOPER

No player has more PGA Tour victories without winning a major than Harry Cooper. Cooper won 31 tournaments during his professional career. He finished second at the 1927 U.S. Open Championship and at the 1936 Masters. His runner-up finish at the 1936 U.S. Open, played at Baltusrol, was his most disheartening. He was leading the tournament on the 16th hole when his approach shot, which was headed for the green, struck a spectator and bounced into a sand trap. Shaken, Cooper bogeyed the hole. Tony Manero shot a final round of 67 for a come-from-behind win.

2. DOUG SANDERS

Doug Sanders's backswing was so short that it was said he could swing in a phone booth. Sanders won 20 times on the

PGA Tour, but never in a major. His best chance came in the 1970 British Open, at St. Andrews. Sanders missed a short putt on the final hole that would have given him the victory. He lost to Jack Nicklaus in a playoff.

3. BRUCE CRAMPTON

Australian Bruce Crampton won 14 tournaments in America, but nary a major. His nemesis was Jack Nicklaus. Crampton was runner-up to the Golden Bear at the 1972 Masters, 1972 U.S. Open Championship, and 1973 and 1975 PGA Championships.

4. COLIN MONTGOMERIE

Colin Montgomerie of Scotland dominated the European Tour, topping the Order of Merit list seven consecutive years during the 1990s. Montgomerie has been frustrated in his quest for a major championship. Twice he finished second in the U.S. Open Championship and was runner-up at the 1995 PGA Championship.

5. JANE BLALOCK

Jane Blalock won 29 tournaments on the LPGA Tour but never finished first in a major. From 1969 to 1980, Blalock played in 289 consecutive tournaments without missing a cut, one of golf's most remarkable records.

6. PHIL MICKELSON

Phil Mickelson is unquestionably the most accomplished left-handed golfer in history. Although he has many years left on the PGA Tour, he has already won nearly 20 tournaments. It seems unlikely that he will finish his career without a major tournament victory.

7. **DAVID DUVAL**

In the late 1990s, David Duval won 11 tournaments over a two-year period. In an era dominated by Tiger Woods, Duval has been ranked number one in the world, and a major victory should only be a matter of time.

8. **BRUCE LIETZKE**

Bruce Lietzke won a dozen tournaments and was a winner on tour in the 1970s, 1980s, and 1990s. The only accomplishment missing from his golf résumé is a victory in a major tournament.

9. **GIL MORGAN**

Gil Morgan won seven tournaments on the PGA Tour between 1977 and 1990. Morgan's best shot at a major was denied when he blew a seven-shot lead at the 1992 U.S. Open Championship. He later became a top player on the Senior Tour.

10. **WAYNE LEVI**

Without much fanfare, Wayne Levi won 12 tournaments on the PGA Tour from 1979 to 1990. He was voted the PGA Tour Player of the Year in 1990, after winning four tournaments. Despite his success, Levi has never captured a major.

Caddie's Corner

A caddie does more than carry a golfer's bag. His or her judgment can make the difference between winning and losing for a professional golfer.

1. BAMBERGER TROPHY CADDIES

Prior to the 1914 Tournament for the Bamberger Trophy, played at the New Siwanoy Golf Club in East Chester, New York, 100 caddies went on strike for higher pay. When replacement caddies were hired, the striking caddies did everything possible to disrupt the tournament. Enraged caddies, wielding golf clubs, hid in the bushes and ambushed replacement caddies and players. Caddies were savagely attacked, while competitors were insulted and harassed. Balls were removed from the fairways and players' golf bags were stolen. Police were brought in to protect the participants. In the end, the caddies were rehired at their old salary of 50 cents per round. They had been seeking a 25-cent raise.

2. SAM SNEAD

Sam Snead had no idea what was in store for him when he traveled to St. Andrews, Scotland, to play in the 1946 British

Open. Used to the well-manicured golf courses in the United States, Snead innocently asked if a links that he saw in St. Andrews was an abandoned golf course. It turned out to be the Royal and Ancient Course on which the tournament was being played. Caddies, insulted by the remark, decided to sabotage Snead's game. As a result, Snead had to hire a different caddie each day. His first caddie whistled when he attempted to putt. The second gave him the wrong clubs. Caddie number three was so drunk that he fell asleep in a bunker. The only caddie who would carry his bag demanded 200 pounds, one-third of the winner's share. Incredibly, despite the distractions, Snead won the tournament by four strokes.

3. **BOB GOALBY**

Bob Goalby, the 1968 Masters champion, had his share of troubles with caddies. At the 1960 Coral Gables Open, in Florida, Goalby needed three putts to win. As his inexperienced seventeen-year-old caddie walked across the putting surface, he accidentally kicked Goalby's ball off the green. Goalby calmly chipped and putted to win the tournament. Five years later, at the 1965 Pensacola Open, Goalby was forced to use an inexperienced caddie when his regular caddie fell ill. At the beginning of the round, Goalby told the caddie to pick up his divots. Later that day, he noticed that the caddie was struggling to carry the bag. The caddie had been picking up the turf divots and placing them in the bag.

4. **AL HOUGHTON**

President Woodrow Wilson's golf game was unexpectedly interrupted during a round at the Bannockburn golf course in Maryland. While Wilson was about to hit a shot, a man ran onto the course and grabbed Wilson's youthful caddie, Al Houghton, by the ear. The man turned out to be a teacher from a nearby school who was sent to bring back the caddie, who was playing hooky. The president convinced the teacher to let him finish the round.

5. EDDIE MARTIN

Byron Nelson lost the 1946 U.S. Open Championship, played at the Canterbury Golf Club in Cleveland, Ohio, when his caddie, Eddie Martin, kicked his ball. The incident happened on the 16th hole during the third round. Martin inadvertently kicked Nelson's ball, which was on the green, incurring a stroke penalty. The miscue proved costly—Nelson lost the championship in a playoff with Lloyd Mangrum.

6. MARK FREIBURG

Curtis Strange, winner of the 1988 and 1989 U.S. Open Championships, was handicapped by a caddie mishap at the 1979 Jackie Gleason Inverrary Classic in Florida. Mark Freiburg, his caddie, lost his balance while crossing the bridge leading to the ninth tee. Strange grabbed Freiburg, but not before most of his golf clubs fell into the water hazard. Strange was forced to finish the round with only four clubs—three irons and a putter. After the round, a diver was hired to retrieve his clubs from the hazard.

7. ROD MUNDAY

Rod Munday's chances of winning at the 1939 Thomasville Open were compromised by a clumsy caddie. The tournament was played at the Glen Arven Country Club in Georgia. On the 18th hole, Munday hit his second shot into a greenside bunker. He asked his caddie to pull the flagstick once he chipped. As the ball rolled toward the cup, the caddie pulled the pin. When he swung the flagstick, he accidentally hit Munday's ball and knocked it into the woods. Munday finished the hole with a quadruple bogey 8.

8. **LEONARD THOMPSON**

Leonard Thompson was teed off after a caddie cost him two strokes at the 1978 Quad Cities Open. Thompson was putting for an eagle when his caddie's exuberance proved disastrous. The caddie stood over the putt, urging it into the cup. Unfortunately, a tee that the caddie had tucked behind his ear fell to the ground right into the path of the ball. The tee not only diverted the ball from its course; Thompson was slapped with a two-stroke penalty.

9. **JACK NICKLAUS**

Jack Nicklaus may have been the greatest golfer in history, but he left something to be desired as a caddie. Nicklaus caddied for his son Gary at the 1983 U.S. Open Championship qualifier, at Hunter's Run Golf Course in Boynton Beach, Florida. Jack realized during the round that he had mistakenly left his own 4-iron in his son's golf bag. The blunder resulted in four penalty strokes, and Gary did not qualify for the Open.

10. **FRED COUPLES**

Jack Nicklaus was not the only professional golfer who failed as a caddie. At the qualifying round for the 1988 K-Mart Greater Greensboro Open, Fred Couples volunteered to caddie for his friend, Tom Patri. On the ninth hole, Couples misidentified a ball in the rough. When Patri hit the wrong ball, he was penalized two strokes. Patri failed to qualify for the tournament.

Streakers and Stalkers

Spectators are an integral part of any golf tournament. Sometimes fans get involved in the play, often with unexpected results.

1. GENE SARAZEN

Gene Sarazen won the 1923 PGA Championship with a helping hand from spectators. Sarazen and Walter Hagen played in the final match on the Pelham Country Club Course in New York. On the 14th hole, Sarazen's ball appeared headed for a pond, but a fan stuck out his foot and stopped it from rolling into the water. Hagen seemed to be a certain winner when Sarazen then hooked his shot over the fence and out of bounds. However, a fan retrieved the ball and threw it back onto the fairway. Spectators, who were rooting for Sarazen, claimed the ball had miraculously bounced back into play. Sarazen, given a second chance, birdied the hole and won the match. Sarazen also won a 1937 Ryder Cup match against Percy Alliss when a woman tossed one of his shots, which landed on her lap, onto the green.

2. **MACDONALD SMITH**

MacDonald Smith actually lost the 1925 British Open because the fans liked him too much. Smith led the Open by five shots going into the final round at Prestwick. The Scottish fans came by the thousands to support their favorite. They crowded so close to him that he could barely swing, and play was delayed several times by overzealous spectators. Smith's concentration was affected by the adulation, and he shot a disappointing final round of 82, falling out of contention. Jim Barnes won the tournament.

3. **JAN STEPHENSON**

Jan Stephenson was one of the most successful golfers on the LPGA Tour—and one of the most attractive. In 1980, a male admirer in her gallery went overboard. The man, who frequently appeared at tournaments in which Stephenson was playing, promised to buy her expensive gifts if she would marry him. The love-smitten fan appeared in various guises, such as an Arab sheik or an Indian chief wearing a headdress.

4. **GARY PLAYER**

Gary Player lost the 1962 Masters because of a handshake. The South African appeared to be on his way to a second consecutive Masters title when he shook hands with a fan with an iron grip. Player sprained his right hand and played the final round with it bandaged. He lost the tournament in a playoff with Arnold Palmer. Two years later, at the 1964 U.S. Open Championship, at the Congressional Country Club in Maryland, he was accidentally pushed into a lake by fans seeking his autograph.

5. **WIFFY COX**

Wiffy Cox had the 1934 U.S. Open Championship, played at the Merion Golf Club in Pennsylvania, pulled out from under him by a fan. On the 12th hole, Cox hit a shot that landed on a spectator's coat lying on the ground. The spectator grabbed the coat, causing the ball to sail out of bounds. Cox finished the tournament two shots behind winner Olin Dutra.

6. **ABE MITCHELL**

Abe Mitchell lost his concentration, and a match, because of an open umbrella. He led John Ball by two strokes at the 1912 British Amateur Championship when they reached the 14th hole at the Westward Ho! Golf Course. Mitchell's approach shot deflected into a sand trap after hitting a spectator's open umbrella. Although unnerved by the bad luck, Mitchell went on to lose the match.

7. **TIGER WOODS**

Tiger Woods does not need lucky bounces, but he received one at the 2000 Canadian Open. During the third round, Woods sliced a tee shot that ricocheted off a young spectator's head and bounced back onto the fairway. Woods won the tournament by one shot over runner-up Grant Waite.

8. **BETTY HICKS**

A cruel joke by a fan cost Betty Hicks the 1953 Nevada Women's Open Championship. Hicks was leading when she hit a shot into a bunker. She was startled to discover that the word "DEATH" had been written in the sand. Disturbed by the message, Hicks shot a 7 on the hole and lost to Patty Berg in a playoff.

9. **FREDDIE TAIT**

Freddie Tait was one of the top golfers in Scotland at the beginning of the twentieth century. Tait was playing a round at the St. Andrews course when he hit a shot through a spectator's hat. The spectator was uninjured, but Tait had to pay him five shillings for a new hat.

10. **PETER JACOBSEN**

Peter Jacobsen tackled a streaker who ran onto the course at the 1985 British Open, played at Royal St. George's in Sandwich, England. Jacobsen finished eleventh in the tournament, which was won by Sandy Lyle.

Unlucky Bounces

Some players have all the bad luck.

1. GREG NORMAN

Greg Norman, the winner of two British Opens, has had a brilliant career, but no golfer has been more victimized by his opponents' great shots. At the 1986 PGA Championship, played at the Inverness Club in Toledo, Ohio, Bob Tway holed out from a bunker on the final hole to edge Norman. The next year at the Masters, Larry Mize chipped in from 140 feet to defeat Norman in a sudden-death playoff. In 1990, Robert Gamez holed a 7-iron shot from 175 yards for an eagle on the 72nd hole, snatching victory from Norman at the Nestle Invitational in Florida. That same year, David Frost made a bunker shot at the USF&G Classic in New Orleans to defeat Norman by one stroke.

2. CRAIG WOOD

Craig Wood was the Greg Norman of his day. Wood appeared on his way to certain victory at the 1935 Masters

when Gene Sarazen made his famous double eagle to wipe
out his lead. Sarazen won the Masters in a playoff. At the
1939 U.S. Open Championship, played at the Spring Mill
Course in Philadelphia, Byron Nelson holed a 1-iron for an
eagle to defeat a stunned Wood in a playoff.

3. **ALEX CAMPBELL**

You could not blame Alex Campbell for feeling deflated after
losing the 1907 U.S. Open Championship, played at the
Philadelphia Cricket Club. Campbell played with a newly
developed pneumatic golf ball, a rubber ball filled with air.
All was going well until Campbell's ball sprung a leak.
Hampered by the deflated ball, Campbell four-putted a crucial hole. He finished three strokes behind winner Alex Ross.

4. **ED DUDLEY**

A perfect drive ruined the chances of Ed Dudley to win the
1937 Masters. Dudley was among the leaders when he teed
off at the 13th hole at Augusta. His drive sailed straight down
the middle of the fairway. Suddenly, a spectator inexplicably
walked out into the path of the shot. The ball bounced off
the spectator's head and into a creek. Dudley double-
bogeyed the hole and finished in third place behind Byron
Nelson.

5. **GENE SARAZEN**

A bit of bad luck knocked Gene Sarazen out of contention at
the 1936 Western Open. His tee shot on a par 3 landed within a few feet of the hole. Unfortunately, the ball ricocheted
off the ball of Jimmy Demaret and rolled into a lake. Sarazen
took a triple-bogey 6 and dropped out of contention.

6. CHARLES MACDONALD

The U.S. Amateur Championship was played at the Newport Golf Club in 1894. The unusual course included a stone quarry in front of the sixth tee and a swamp running up the left side of the second hole. The oddest features of the course were stone walls that cut across some of the fairways. Charles Macdonald hit a ball right down the center of the fairway only to have it lodge against one of the walls. He incurred a two-shot penalty and lost the tournament by one stroke to W. G. Lawrence.

7. JOHNNY MILLER

Johnny Miller needed only a par 5 on the final hole to win the 1973 Atlanta Open. His drive struck a spectator's chair on the edge of the fairway and bounced out of bounds. Miller's misfortune allowed Jack Nicklaus to win the tournament.

8. JIM WOODWARD

Jim Woodward looked like he was on course for his first tournament victory at the 1992 GTE Byron Nelson Classic, played at the Colinas Golf Course in Texas. During the final round, he birdied the first two holes to take the lead at 12 under par. Rain suspended play and the final round was eventually canceled. Scores reverted to the 54-hole totals and Woodward finished fifth, one shot behind Billy Ray Brown, who won in a four-man playoff.

9. PETER ALLISS

Thirteen proved to be an unlucky number for Peter Alliss at the 1961 World Match Play Championship. Alliss lost to Harold Henning on the 13th playoff hole.

10. **BOB MAY**

Bob May picked the wrong time to play the greatest golf of his life. May, who had never won on the PGA Tour, shot 66 in each of his final three rounds at the 2000 PGA Championship, played at the Valhalla Golf Course in Louisville, Kentucky. Despite his inspired play, May lost the tournament in a playoff to Tiger Woods.

Disqualified

H ere are some of the most outrageous disqualifications in golf history.

1. **ROBERTO DE VICENZO**

Roberto De Vicenzo won 250 tournaments around the world, but he will always be remembered for the one he lost. He finished the 1968 Masters tournament in a tie with Bob Goalby. The Argentine golfer hoped to celebrate his forty-fifth birthday with his first Masters win. However, he never got the opportunity to be in a playoff with Goalby. After his round, De Vicenzo was informed that he had signed an incorrect scorecard. His playing partner, Tommy Aaron, had marked down a par 4 on the 17th hole, when De Vicenzo had actually scored a birdie 3. According to the rules, De Vicenzo was forced to accept the score on his card. Instead of a final round of 65, he was credited with a 66. Bob Goalby was declared the winner, and De Vicenzo was relegated to the runner-up position.

2. **PORKY OLIVER**

Porky Oliver lost his chance to win the 1940 U.S. Open Championship, played at the Canterbury Golf Club in Cleveland, Ohio, because he teed off too soon. He was one of six golfers who began playing before their scheduled tee time because of threatening weather. Oliver finished the tournament in a tie for the lead with Lawson Little and Byron Nelson but was disqualified for teeing off out of order.

3. **FRED ROWLAND**

Fred Rowland was disqualified from the 1988 British Amateur Championship, played in Porthcawl, Wales, before he teed off. Moments before he was to begin his round, the American realized he had to answer a call of nature. After paying a visit to a portable toilet, Rowland returned to discover that his playing partner had already teed off. Rowland was informed that he had been disqualified for not being present when his name was called.

4. **DOUG SANDERS**

Doug Sanders shot 67 in the second round of the 1966 Pensacola Open in Florida to open up a four-shot lead. The popular golfer was mobbed by fans and graciously signed dozens of autographs. The one thing he forgot to sign was his scorecard. Sanders was disqualified for this oversight, and Gay Brewer went on to win the tournament.

5. **CRAIG STADLER**

Craig Stadler felt like throwing in the towel after he was disqualified at the 1987 Andy Williams Open, played at the Torrey Pines Golf Course in La Jolla, California. During the third round, Stadler hit a ball under a group of palm trees on the 14th hole. He was forced to kneel to hit the shot beneath the low-hanging branches. He placed a towel on the ground to prevent his pants from getting muddy. Only after Stadler had signed his scorecard did he learn that he had been assessed a two-stroke penalty for improving his stance. Because he signed an incorrect scorecard, Stadler was disqualified.

6. JOHN PANTON

John Panton decided he needed some extra practice between rounds of the 1946 British Open. After play had concluded, he went on the St. Andrews course and practiced his putting. He was disqualified when tournament officials discovered that he was practicing on the tournament course, an infraction of the rules.

7. JOHN MCMULLIN

John McMullin was disqualified for two separate incidents at the 1960 Motor City Open, in Detroit, Michigan. McMullin took a practice swing in a sand trap on the seventh hole, incurring a penalty. On the 14th hole, he was assessed another penalty for striking a ball still in motion. McMullin added one penalty shot on each hole and signed his scorecard, but he was disqualified. McMullin later learned that he should have added two penalty strokes on each hole.

8. WAYNE GRADY

Wayne Grady was disqualified twice in 1986 for hitting the wrong ball in PGA tournaments. Grady's failure to identify his own ball resulted in disqualifications at the Phoenix and Los Angeles Opens.

9. **DAVID EISNER**

David Eisner's scoring errors resulted in two of his playing partners being disqualified at the 1971 U.S. Publinx Championship. He wrote down the wrong score for Larry Castagnoli during the first round, and Castagnoli was disqualified for signing an incorrect card. The following day, the same thing happened to playing partner Fred Lufkin. Although Eisner's scorecard was correct, he failed to make the cut.

10. **DAVE HILL**

Dave Hill's temper got the best of him at the 1971 Colonial Open, in Fort Worth, Texas. Angered because he hit a ball into a bunker on the 12th hole, Hill picked up the ball and tossed it like a basketball shot onto the green. He marked down a 2 for the hole and was disqualified and fined $500 for his action.

Preposterous Penalties

Even the best golfers are occasionally assessed penalties. Nick Faldo, a three-time British Open champion, was penalized on two consecutive days at the 1994 British Open for hitting other players' balls.

1. PAUL FARMER

Halfway through the third round of the 1960 Texas Open, played at the Fort Sam Houston Golf Course in San Antonio, Paul Farmer decided to change putters. Once he completed his round, Farmer was horrified to discover that he had been penalized 18 strokes, two per hole, for changing clubs. The rules state that a golfer can change putters during a round only if a club is damaged. Instead of shooting a 70, Farmer was credited with a round of 88.

2. JACK FLECK

At the 1960 Western Open, Jack Fleck hit a shot into a water hazard. Deciding that the ball was playable, Fleck took four practice swings before playing the shot. Penalized two strokes for each practice swing within the hazard, Fleck finished the hole with a 13.

3. **BOB DICKSON**

Bob Dickson paid the price for having one too many clubs in his bag at the 1965 U.S. Amateur Championship. During a round, he discovered that he had 15 clubs in his bag, one over the limit. It turned out that another player had placed his club in Dickson's bag by mistake. Dickson notified tournament officials and was penalized four shots.

4. **J. C. SNEAD**

A bizarre occurrence cost J. C. Snead two strokes at the 1977 Players Championship, played at the Sawgrass Golf Course in Ponte Vedra, Florida. On the fourth hole, a sudden gust of wind blew off Snead's Panama hat. The hat skipped down the fairway and struck his ball, which was safely on the green. Snead was penalized two shots for "putting" with his hat. The rules state that only standard golfing equipment can be used for putting.

5. **ANDY BEAN**

Andy Bean lost the 1983 Canadian Open by making a putt. During the third round, Bean made a two-inch putt using the grip of his club. He was penalized two strokes for not using the blade of the putter. The next day, Bean shot a 62 but lost the tournament by two shots, the number of strokes he had been penalized.

6. **DOW FINSTERWALD**

A practice putt cost Dow Finsterwald his chance to win the 1962 Masters. During the first round, he missed a short putt to the fifth hole. Before he left the green, he took a practice putt. Finsterwald incurred a two-stroke penalty and finished the tournament in a tie with Gary Player and Arnold Palmer. The penalty was disastrous, as Palmer won the playoff.

7. **MARK BROOKS**

Mark Brooks tossed away two strokes on the final hole of the 1991 Las Vegas International. Brooks hit the ball safely onto the green. He marked the ball and tossed it to his caddie. The caddie missed the ball, and it rolled into a water hazard. Brooks climbed into the hazard and found eighteen golf balls but could not locate his own. He was given a two-stroke penalty for the lost ball and finished his round with a 78.

8. **LLOYD MANGRUM**

Lloyd Mangrum lost the 1950 U.S. Open Championship, played at the Merion Golf Course in Pennsylvania, because of a gnat. He was ready to putt when a gnat landed on his ball. Without thinking, Mangrum picked up his ball to swat away the gnat. Assessed a two-stroke penalty, Mangrum lost the tournament in a playoff to Ben Hogan.

9. **ROGER WETHERED**

Roger Wethered lost the 1921 British Open because he was not watching where he was walking. He was lining up a putt on the 14th hole at St. Andrews when he stepped on his own ball. The one-stroke penalty made all the difference— Wethered lost a playoff to Jock Hutchison.

10. **FRAN WADSWORTH**

Fran Wadsworth proved that a golfer could hit two balls with one shot at the 1986 U.S. Open Championship, played at the Shinnecock Hills Golf Club in Southampton, New York. On the third hole, Wadsworth hit his shot from the fairway, not aware that another ball was imbedded in the soft ground beneath his ball. Both balls sailed down the fairway. Confused, Wadsworth hit the wrong ball on his next shot and incurred a two-stroke penalty. He completed the hole with a triple-bogey 7.

Rounds They Would Rather Forget

E ven the best golfers have off days.

1. **KEL NAGLE**

Kel Nagle was in second place after the first round of the 1969 Alcan Golfer of the Year Tournament, in Portland, Oregon. The next day he shot 35 on both nines, for a round of 70. Nagle's marker mistakenly wrote the nine-hole total of 35 as his score for the ninth hole. Nagle signed the incorrect scorecard and was forced to add the additional strokes to his score, dropping him from near the top of the leader board to last place.

2. **MICKEY WRIGHT**

Mickey Wright was a Hall of Fame golfer, but she had a nightmare round at the 1957 Tampa Women's Open, in Florida. She was penalized 24 strokes for carrying an extra club in her bag for 12 holes. With the penalty strokes added in, Wright shot a horrendous 104.

3. **SERGIO GARCIA**

Sergio Garcia is considered one of the best young golfers in the world, but you would not know it from the way he played at the 1999 British Open. The promising Spaniard shot an 89 in the first round of the Open, played at Carnoustie in Scotland.

4. **AL BALDING**

Al Balding was tied for the lead going into the final round of the 1964 Bing Crosby National Pro-Am. On a windy, rainy day, Balding shot an 88 to fall from contention. Tony Lema won the tournament despite a final round of 76.

5. **JOHN DALY**

John Daly is the longest driver on the PGA Tour and a major tournament winner. However, he has had his share of bad rounds. At the 1999 U.S. Open Championship, played at Pinehurst in North Carolina, Daly shot an 11 on the fourth hole during a round of 83. The following year, in the first round of the 2000 U.S. Open, played at Pebble Beach, Daly scored a 14 on the 18th hole, shooting another 83.

6. **JACK NICKLAUS**

The great Jack Nicklaus shot 83 in the first round of the 1981 British Open, at the Royal St. George's Golf Course. The next day, he redeemed himself by firing an outstanding round of 66.

7. **DONNIE HAMMOND**

At the 1983 Bay Hill Classic, Donnie Hammond was among the leaders when he shot a 32 on the front nine. On the 10th tee, playing partner Jack Nicklaus excused himself to answer a call of nature in the locker room. Hammond hit out of turn and was penalized two strokes. Unnerved by the penalty, he shot a 48 on the back nine and dropped to fortieth place.

8. DON JANUARY

Don January was one of four golfers suspended for 30 days for intentionally shooting a high round. January, George Bayer, Ernie Vossler, and Doug Higgins deliberately played poorly in the third round of the 1957 Kentucky Derby Open, because they were not allowed to withdraw after making the cut.

9. MAURICE FLITCROFT

The qualifiers for the major championships bring together some of the best golfers in the world. A notable exception occurred at a qualifier for the 1976 British Open. Englishman Maurice Flitcroft decided to enter even though he had never played a round of golf. Flitcroft shot 121 on the Formby, Lancashire, course, the worst score ever shot in the qualifying round of the British Open. The championship committee, embarrassed that they had allowed Flitcroft to play, refunded the entry fee of his playing partners. Flitcroft wisely withdrew prior to the second round.

10. BOBBY JONES

Bobby Jones is the only man ever to win golf's Grand Slam, but he was no match for Walter Hagen in a 1928 exhibition. Jones lost 12 and 11 in the 72-hole match.

Golf's Most Embarrassing Moments

These golfers learned the hard way that golf can be an embarrassing game.

1. TOMMY BOLT

Tommy Bolt was notorious for his temper, but the fine he incurred at the 1959 Memphis Invitational Open was for passing gas. As his playing partner was about to putt, Bolt broke wind. Terrible Tommy was fined $250 for unsportsmanlike conduct.

2. JOHNNY MCDERMOTT

Johnny McDermott was the U.S. Open champion in 1911 and 1912. McDermott traveled to Prestwick, Scotland, in an attempt to qualify for the 1914 British Open. He arrived at Prestwick only to discover that the qualifying rounds had been held the previous week. McDermott was unable to compete in the tournament won by Harry Vardon.

3. **STEVE MELNYK**

Steve Melnyk flew 4,000 miles to Hawaii to compete in a professional tournament. Upon arrival, he was informed that he had forgotten to enter the event and could not compete.

4. **BECKY LARSON**

Becky Larson holds the dubious distinction of missing the cut in 88 consecutive LPGA tournaments between 1985 and 1990. In September 1990, Larson finally survived the cut of the Rail Charity Golf Classic in Springfield, Illinois. After going five years without earning a dime on the tour, Larson received a check for $283.

5. **KENT KLUBA AND RAPHAEL ALARCON**

At the 1985 French Open, Kent Kluba and his playing partner, Raphael Alarcon, played through without even knowing it. The golfers completed the second hole and walked to what they thought was the third tee. Only after they had teed off did they learn that they were playing the 13th hole instead of the third. They had skipped 10 holes.

6. **AL CHANDLER**

Al Chandler whiffed not once, not twice, but three times on a single hole at the 1986 Senior Tournament Players Championship, at the Canterbury Country Club near Cleveland, Ohio. On the 15th hole, Chandler hit a shot that landed next to an oak tree. He missed the ball twice while attempting to chip onto the green. Chandler's misadventures continued when he whiffed on a tap-in putt.

7. JOHNNY MILLER

Johnny Miller was known as one of the most accurate golfers in history, but he hit three errant shots on the 17th hole of the final round of the 1982 Memorial Tournament, played at the Muirfield Village Golf Course in Dublin, Ohio. Only one shot behind the leader, Miller hit three consecutive shots off the same pine tree and triple-bogeyed the hole. Miller's lapse dropped him to twenty-second place.

8. HOT ROD HUNDLEY

Hot Rod Hundley was a colorful basketball player who was a member of the Los Angeles Lakers from 1957 to 1963. Hundley played at the 1986 Showdown Classic Pro-Am, at the Jeremy Ranch Golf Club in Park City, Utah. Hundley popped up his tee shot straight into the air. Hot Rod nonchalantly reached up and caught his own drive.

9. R. R. SMILEY

In 1939, R. R. Smiley hit a hole-in-one on the 11th hole of a golf course in Goldsboro, North Carolina. The bad news was that he was playing the 13th hole at the time. Smiley sliced the shot, which landed on the 11th green and rolled into the wrong hole.

10. HILLARY RODHAM CLINTON

President Bill Clinton tried to interest his wife, Hillary, in the game of golf, one of his favorite pastimes. In 1994, the first lady agreed to play nine holes at the Mink Meadows Golf

Club on Martha's Vineyard, in Massachusetts. On the first swing, Hillary missed the ball entirely, taking up a huge divot. Her second drive sailed straight up into the air. Finally, on the third try, Hillary tapped the ball 75 yards down the fairway.

Moe, Muffin, and Mysterious Montague

H ere is a gallery of some of golf's most distinctive personalities.

1. MOE NORMAN

Moe Norman was a fine Canadian golfer who may have been even better had he not been the shyest player on record. Following a victory at the 1955 Canadian Amateur Championship, Norman hid in the bushes during the trophy presentation because he was too shy to face the spectators assembled at the 18th green. He withdrew after the second round of the 1956 Masters because he claimed the crowd made him nervous. He insisted on carrying his own bag, claiming that it was not heavy. Before a tournament began, Norman would pick what place in the standings he felt he deserved and would play just well enough to finish there. He occasionally made side bets with spectators on the outcome of his shots. In one tournament, Norman needed three putts on the final hole to win. He intentionally putted off the green, then chipped and putted for the win. At the Los Angeles Open, Norman used a Coke bottle as a tee on one of the holes.

2. **JOHN MONTAGUE**

During the 1930s, John Montague was one of the best golfers on the West Coast. Montague once bet Bing Crosby, himself a scratch golfer, that he could beat him on a hole using a baseball bat, shovel, and rake. On the par 4 10th hole at the Lakeside Country Club in North Hollywood, Montague drove the ball 350 yards using a baseball bat. He chipped out of a sand trap to within five feet of the cup using a shovel. Then he raked the ball into the hole for a birdie 3 to best Crosby by one shot.

He was nicknamed Mysterious Montague because he avoided publicity and refused to let photographers take his picture. Once Montague even refused to play the final hole of a round, fearful that he might break the course record. In 1937, it was discovered that his real name was Laverne Moore and that he was a suspect in a 1930 robbery. Montague was tried for his alleged involvement in the crime but was acquitted.

3. **WALTER HAGEN**

The winner of 11 major tournaments, Walter Hagen loved the high life. He once said, "I never wanted to be a millionaire; I just wanted to live like one." He contracted food poisoning while eating a lobster dinner the night before the 1914 U.S. Open Championship and then miraculously went out and won the tournament. The night before the final round of the 1919 U.S. Open, Hagen stayed out partying all night, yet still won the tournament. Once he arrived late at the tee wearing a tuxedo. Hagen would wear his pants only one time and sometimes gave them as tips to bellhops. In New York, he drove golf balls out of his hotel room overlooking Central Park. The master of gamesmanship, Hagen would walk to the tee and ask loudly, "I wonder who's going to finish second."

4. GARY MCCORD

Gary McCord has been a colorful personality as both a golfer and a golf commentator. His original sponsor on the PGA Tour was bandleader Lawrence Welk. At the 1984 Memphis Open, McCord's tight pants split, and he had to finish the round wearing another golfer's rain pants. He played a round at the 1977 Heritage Classic in just 87 minutes. McCord's off-the-wall comments got him banned from the announcing booth at the Masters.

5. ANDY BEAN

Andy Bean, a three-time winner of the Doral Open, between 1977 and 1986, was one of the PGA Tour's most entertaining players. Bean won $50 bets by biting covers off golf balls. He also once wrestled an alligator he spotted on a golf course in Florida.

6. MUFFIN SPENCER-DEVLIN

Muffin Spencer-Devlin won three tournaments on the LPGA Tour in the 1980s. In addition to being a golfer, she was a model, actress, writer, and television personality. A believer in reincarnation, Spencer-Devlin was convinced that she had been King Arthur in a previous life.

7. MARK JAMES

Mark James has been one of Great Britain's best golfers for the past quarter century. In the late 1970s, James experienced trouble with his putting. He was certain that his putter was possessed by an evil spirit. In an attempt to purge the putter of its demons, he kicked it and threw it into the bushes of a car park.

8. **CHI CHI RODRIGUEZ**

Chi Chi Rodriguez has won eight tournaments on the PGA Tour and more than 20 more on the Senior Tour. One of golf's most colorful performers, Rodriguez often made swordlike movements with his putter after sinking a putt. Also, he placed his hat over the cup to make sure the ball did not escape. In 1966, while playing a round at the Dorado Beach Country Club in Puerto Rico, Chi Chi bet a playing companion that he would give him two strokes on a hole if he was given a throw. The golfer believed he was a sure winner when they both reached the green in regulation. Rodriguez informed the man that he was ready to use his throw. He picked up his opponent's ball and threw it into the ocean.

9. **LEE TREVINO**

The "Merry Mex," Lee Trevino was known for his pranks. In 1971, he and Jack Nicklaus competed in a playoff for the U.S. Open Championship, at Merion Golf Club in Pennsylvania. On the first tee, Trevino threw a rubber snake at Nicklaus and then danced around with the snake on his clubhead. Trevino shot a 68 and won the playoff by three shots.

10. **PETER JACOBSEN**

Peter Jacobsen has one of the best senses of humor in golf. He is adept at imitating other players, from their swings to their mannerisms.

African American Stars

Tiger Woods is golf's first African American superstar. Like other sports, professional golf was segregated for many years. The PGA Tour did not remove their Caucasian clause, which excluded African American golfers as members, from its constitution until 1961. These golfers helped pave the way for Woods's success.

1. CHARLIE SIFFORD

Charlie Sifford shot a 64 in the final round to win the 1967 Greater Hartford Open, becoming the first African American to win an event on the PGA Tour. Two years later, at the age of forty-six, he won the Los Angeles Open. Sifford won the 1975 PGA Seniors' Championship and earned nearly a million dollars on the Senior Tour.

2. JOHN SHIPPEN

One of the best early African American golfers, John Shippen was only 16 years old when he played in his first U.S. Open Championship in 1896, at Shinnecock Hills in New York. Many of the professionals, reflecting the prejudice of the day, threatened to withdraw if Shippen was allowed to play. However, USGA President Theodore Havermeyer declared that the tournament would go on even if Shippen was the only participant. Shippen was tied for the lead after the first round, only to have disaster strike at the 13th hole of the second round. His shot landed on a sandy road. The sand wedge had not yet been invented, and it was next to impossible to hit a shot from the sand. Shippen took an 11 on the hole and finished in fifth place, seven strokes behind the winner, James Foulis. He earned $10 for his fifth-place finish. Shippen also finished fifth at the 1902 U.S. Open, played at Garden City, New York. Shippen later earned a living as a private golf instructor to wealthy men, such as steel magnate Henry Clay Frick.

3. **LEE ELDER**

Lee Elder was responsible for breaking the color barrier at the Masters. He qualified for the 1975 Masters by winning the 1974 Monsanto Open. Elder won several tournaments on the PGA Tour, including the Houston Open, the Greater Milwaukee Open, and the Westchester Classic. On the Senior Tour, Elder won eight tournaments and set a record for the lowest round in tour history when he shot a 61 during the 1985 Merrill Lynch/Golf Digest Commemorative, played at the Newport Country Club in Rhode Island.

4. **CALVIN PEETE**

The most successful African American golfer on the PGA Tour prior to Tiger Woods was Calvin Peete. He won a dozen tournaments between 1979 and 1986, capped off by a victory in the 1986 Tournament Players Championship. One of the straightest drivers in golf history, he led the PGA Tour in driving accuracy for 10 consecutive years, beginning in 1981.

5. JOSEPH BARTHOLOMEW

Joseph Bartholomew excelled as both a golfer and a course architect. He was good enough to defeat Freddie McLeod, the 1908 U.S. Open Championship winner, in many matches. McLeod hired Bartholomew as an assistant professional at the Audubon Club. In the 1920s, Bartholomew built three courses in the New Orleans area and several courses in Louisiana and Mississippi. Although Bartholomew built the courses and was a club professional, he was not permitted a single round on them and was not paid a cent for designing any of the New Orleans courses. However, through shrewd investments in construction, insurance, manufacturing, and real estate, he earned a fortune. Bartholomew built a seven-hole course for African American golfers on his own property in Harahan, Louisiana.

6. PETE BROWN

Pete Brown was the first African American to win a PGA-sponsored event, the 1963 Waco Turner Open, in Texas. In 1970, Brown won a PGA Tour event, the Andy Williams San Diego Open.

7. DEWEY BROWN

In 1928, Dewey Brown became the first African American member of the Professional Golfers' Association. However, he was expelled in 1934 when it was learned that the light-skinned golfer was actually African American.

8. JIM THORPE

In 1985, Jim Thorpe won the Greater Milwaukee Open and the Tucson Match Play Championship. After turning 50, Thorpe won more than $2 million on the Senior Tour.

9. BILL SPILLER

At the 1952 San Diego Open, Bill Spiller was not permitted to compete. In protest, Spiller stood on the first tee and delayed the start of play. His protest helped bring attention to the injustice of excluding African American golfers from tournaments.

10. BILL WRIGHT

Bill Wright, of Seattle, Washington, was the first African American to win an event sponsored by the United States Golf Association. Wright won the 1959 United States Amateur Public Links Tournament, played at the Welshire Golf Club in Denver, Colorado.

Friendly Wagers

Betting on golf has always been a popular diversion. During the 1930s, pari-mutuel betting was permitted at the Agua Caliente Open in California. As a youth in Texas, Lee Trevino made money betting golfers he could defeat them by playing with a taped Dr Pepper bottle. Two-time PGA Champion Leo Diegel frequently won bets that he could shoot 75 or under while playing on one leg. Napoleon Whitehead, a caddie for Dwight Eisenhower, once bet his caddie fee on the president. When Eisenhower left a 20-footer 10 feet short, Whitehead admonished the chief executive, "For Christ's sake, Mr. President, hit it."

1. BOBBY CRUICKSHANK

Golfer Bobby Cruickshank was so certain that Bobby Jones was going to win the Grand Slam that he bet on it. Cruickshank claimed he bet $100 and won $10,000 on the wager. However, the *New York Times* reported that he won $108,000.

2. **BILL SPILLER**

Outstanding African American golfer Bill Spiller once played an all-day golf match with heavyweight boxing champion Joe Louis. Louis, who on his best day could shoot in the 70s, liked to bet while playing golf. By the end of the day, Spiller had won enough money from the Brown Bomber to buy a house.

3. **HOWARD HUGHES**

Billionaire Howard Hughes was a scratch golfer who often bet on his matches. Although he did not need the money, he hated to lose a wager. Once, during a match in Los Angeles, his playing partners were about to putt when one of the starlets Hughes had under contract at his movie studio walked totally nude onto a balcony overlooking the course. The distraction worked as planned—the golfers missed their putts and Hughes won the bet.

4. **JOHN F. KENNEDY**

Although he was a wealthy man and an excellent golfer, John F. Kennedy preferred to make small side bets during his rounds. He often bet 10 cents a hole, along with similar side bets on the longest drive, closest to the pin, and first in the hole. Rarely did more than $5 change hands during a match. When playing partner General Chester Clinton missed a four-foot putt to cost them a match, Kennedy quipped, "Nice putt, Sergeant."

5. **TIGER WOODS**

At age four, Tiger Woods came off a golf course with a pocketful of quarters. When his father, Earl, asked him where he got them, Tiger replied that he had won them putting against older boys playing in a junior tournament. His father opposed gambling and told him, "I don't want you playing for quarters anymore." Tiger listened to his father's advice. The next time, he returned with his pockets full of dollar bills.

6. BRYAN FIELD

Bryan Field had not played golf in years when he decided to play a round at the Pine Valley Golf Course, in June 1950. The New Jersey course is among the world's most difficult. A friend bet Field that he could not play the course in less than 300 strokes. Field struggled to a round of 148 but still won the wager by 152 shots.

7. TITANIC THOMPSON

Alvin "Titanic" Thompson won a small fortune winning bets from unsuspecting golfers. He offered to play left-handed, not telling them that he was a natural southpaw. Thompson watered the greens to create paths so that he could make long putts. He once bet someone he could hit a drive 500 yards and won the wager by driving a ball onto a frozen lake. One of Thompson's favorite ploys was to bet that he could beat a golfer after allowing him to hit three drives on each hole and play the best one. He realized that golfers would soon get tired and lose the later holes. In 1935, Thompson won a $10,000 wager with a clever trick. He instructed his caddie to drop a $10 bill in a sand trap next to his playing companion's ball. When the man picked up the money, Thompson assessed him a stroke penalty for removing an object from the hazard before hitting his shot. The flustered golfer lost the bet. Thompson even bet that his caddie could beat his opponents. He hired up-and-coming golfers to caddie for him and almost always won his wagers. Well-known players who caddied for Thompson included Horton Smith, Ky Laffoon, and Lee Elder.

8. FREDDIE TAIT

Scottish golfer Freddie Tait bet that he could hit a golf ball from Royal St. George's Golf Course to Royal Cinque Ports Golf Club, a distance of three miles, in less than 40 shots. Tait won the bet when his thirty-second shot sailed through the clubhouse window.

9. SAM SNEAD

Fifty-five-year-old Sam Snead was paired with twenty-year-old tour rookie Bobby Cole during a practice round at the 1967 Masters. The two men bet a $5 nassau on the round. They were tied on the par-5 13th hole when Cole was faced with playing a ball over tall pine trees guarding the green. Snead remarked, "Bobby, when I was your age I could knock a ball over those trees." Cole attempted the shot, only to hit one of the branches. "How did you do it?" he asked. With a smile on his face, Snead replied, "When I was your age those trees were only 20 feet high." Thanks to the deception, Snead won the bet.

10. DWIGHT EISENHOWER

Golf enthusiast Dwight Eisenhower enjoyed making small bets during a round. While president, he played a match with Bob Hope, General Omar Bradley, and Senator Stuart Symington. On the first tee, Eisenhower said, "I just loaned Bolivia $2 million, I'll play for a dollar nassau."

Losing Your Temper

Golf can be a frustrating game, and golfers frequently lose their temper. Even-tempered Gerald Ford once wrapped his driver around a tee box after slicing a shot, and he was even given a trophy by friends for the longest putter throw.

1. LEFTY STACKHOUSE

Lefty Stackhouse, a top professional player of the 1930s and 1940s, had an uncontrollable temper. After hitting a bad shot, he would punish whatever part of his body had let him down. After misreading a putt, he would bang his head against a tree or smash it against his putter. Once, when he hooked a drive, he stuck his hand into a rosebush until it was torn open by the thorns. Another time, when he missed a crucial putt at a tournament, he punched himself so hard that he knocked himself out. And following a round of 80 during a tournament in Houston, he threw himself into a hedge of rosebushes. When he was not abusing himself, he was destroying his clubs and golf bag in fits of anger. In one of his most notorious rages, he threw his golf clubs, bag, *and* caddie into a water hazard.

2. KY LAFFOON

A contemporary of Lefty Stackhouse, Ky Laffoon was his equal on the golf course and in temper tantrums. He specialized in blaming his clubs for errant shots. Following one poor tournament, Laffoon dragged his putter behind his car for 400 miles to teach it a lesson. At the Jacksonville Open in Florida, he missed a short putt on the 16th hole. Enraged, he began choking the putter. Not satisfied, he tried to drown the club in an adjoining creek. After finishing a bad hole, he would spit tobacco juice into the cup. During the Sacramento Open in California, he missed a five-foot putt and became so enraged that he slammed the club into his foot. For his trouble, he broke the shaft and one of his toes.

3. CLAYTON HEAFNER

Clayton Heafner was another golfer who had trouble controlling his temper. On the first tee of the 1941 Oakland Open, in California, Heafner stalked off the course after the public address announcer mispronounced his name. He was known to charge into crowds and attack heckling spectators. After shooting a round of 81, Heafner took out his frustration on his Model T Ford. He shattered the window, tore off the doors, slashed the upholstery, and dismantled the engine.

4. TOMMY BOLT

Terrible Tommy Bolt, the 1958 United States Open champion, did not hit many bad shots, but when he did, everyone had better duck. Bolt was infamous for throwing clubs. Many of them ended up in water hazards. In 1957, the PGA passed the "Tommy Bolt" rule, which penalized any player throwing a club. When Bolt was not tossing clubs, he was breaking them. During the 1953 Tournament of Champions, in Las Vegas, he broke both his putter and driver in the same round. In 1962, Bolt walked off the course in the middle of a round at the Philadelphia Classic because the gallery had not applauded one of his better tee shots.

5. IVAN GANTZ

Ivan Gantz was referred to as "Ivan The Terrible" because of his short fuse. In reaction to a poor shot, he might hit himself in the forehead with a club or rock. Fans were stunned when he would roll in the fairway in a rage. Gantz once threw himself facedown into a bunker in the midst of a temper tantrum.

6. WAYNE LEVI

Wayne Levi was the 1990 PGA Player of the Year, but one of his less glorious moments occurred during a qualifying round for the 1977 U.S. Open Championship. Levi drove out of bounds on the 17th hole. Feeling that his driver had betrayed him, Levi attempted to strangle the club. While shaking the club, he hit himself in the mouth, splitting his lip. Bothered by the fat lip, Levi had a bad round and did not qualify for the Open.

7. CYRIL WALKER

Cyril Walker, winner of the 1924 U.S. Open Championship, was notorious for his slow play. At the 1930 Los Angeles Open, played at the Riviera Country Club, he was disqualified on the ninth hole for taking too much time between shots. Walker refused to leave the course and was dragged away, kicking and screaming, by officers of the Los Angeles police force.

8. **MARK MCNULTY**

Mark McNulty was undone by an inconsiderate fan at the 1979 Japanese Open. During the third round, McNulty missed a short putt when he was distracted by a fan trying to find a seat in the grandstand. A few moments later, McNulty missed another short putt when that same fan dropped a lunch box. Angered, McNulty broke his putter across his knee. Forced to putt with his 1-iron, McNulty shot a 77.

9. **GREG NORMAN**

Greg Norman lost his temper at the 1987 Kemper Open, played at the TPC-Avenel Course in Potomac, Maryland. Reacting to a bad shot, Norman tried to throw his ball into a water hazard but instead struck playing partner Fred Couples square in the chest.

10. **BOBBY JONES**

Early in his career, Bobby Jones had trouble controlling his temper. The young golfer frequently threw clubs or broke them in half. His lowest moment came during the third round of the 1921 British Open, at St. Andrews. Jones was stewing after shooting a 46 on the front nine. On the 11th hole, he hit a ball into a bunker. Still in the trap after four more shots, Jones walked off the course and tore up his scorecard.

Birdies and the Bees

Birdies and eagles are not the only animals golfers encounter during play.

1. TED BARNHOUSE

Ted Barnhouse made an improbable hole-in-one in 1981 on the fourth hole of the Mountain View Country Club course in John Day, Oregon. His drive bounced off the head of a cow that was standing in the fairway. The ball then ricocheted off a lawn mower and rolled into the cup. Ironically, Barnhouse earned his living as a cattle rancher.

2. A. WHEDDEN

In 1928, a golfer identified as A. Whedden made a hole-in-one with the help of a lamb. The assisted ace occurred at the Burton-on-Trent course in England. Whedden's tee shot came to rest a few feet from the hole. A lamb, grazing on the green, picked up the ball and dropped it into the cup.

3. P. M. GREGOR

P. M. Gregor of Kirkfield, Ontario, won a match in 1921 because of a grasshopper. Gregor needed to make a long putt to win. He was disappointed when his putt hung on the lip of the cup. At that moment, a grasshopper landed on the ball and its weight was enough to push the ball into the hole.

4. H. J. MORLAND

The old saying goes, The early bird catches the worm, but H. J. Morland discovered, to his regret, that occasionally the worm gets the birdie. In 1951, Morland was putting for a birdie 4 during a round in Phoenix, Arizona. He was dumbfounded when his putt suddenly stopped inches short of the hole. When he examined the ball, Morland was surprised to find that an earthworm had wrapped itself around it.

5. MICHAEL MCEVOY

Michael McEvoy was victimized by an animal during a 1922 round at The Middleton Golf Club in Cork, Ireland. On the third hole, he hit a drive that stuck in the ear of a donkey grazing on the fairway. The startled animal ran off the course. McEvoy located the ball in the woods and played out for a double-bogey 6.

6. LAWSON LITTLE

Lawson Little, the 1940 U.S. Open champion, had what only can be described as a catastrophe during a round at St. Andrews on May 4, 1934. Little hit his ball onto the 17th green, the famed Road Hole. However, before he could reach the green, a Persian cat picked up the ball and ran off. Little was permitted to replace the ball on the green.

7. DWIGHT EISENHOWER

When he was president, Dwight Eisenhower had a putting green built on the White House lawn. He became irritated when squirrels kept digging it up. Eisenhower ordered the Secret Service to shoot any squirrel seen on the putting surface. Instead, they trapped the animals and transported them to Rock Creek Park.

8. WIFFY COX

Wiffy Cox, the head professional at the Congressional Country Club near Washington, D.C., shot more than birdies in 1939. Cox shot 33 skunks that had been digging up the course.

9. W. J. ROBINSON

In 1934, W. J. Robinson hit a killer drive on the 18th hole at the Kent Golf Course in England. His tee shot struck and killed a cow grazing on the course.

10. LLAMA CADDIES

When The Talamore Golf Course opened in Pinehurst, North Carolina, in 1991, it offered golfers an interesting alternative. Golfers could choose to have a llama as their caddie. Each animal was capable of carrying two golf bags and cost $200 per round.

Wild and Dangerous

S ometimes golf can be like big-game hunting.

1. RICHARD BLACKMAN

Richard Blackman and his playing partner William Smithline never expected what they encountered at the 16th hole of the Paradise Island Golf Course in Nassau, Bahamas. The golfers ran for their lives when they were chased by a lion that had escaped from a circus. The lion was recaptured and the players escaped unharmed.

2. JIMMY STEWART

Jimmy Stewart, the golfer not the actor, found more than his ball in the grass at the 1972 Singapore Open. A 10-foot cobra, which had apparently mistaken his ball for an egg, was coiled on the fairway. Stewart used an iron to kill the deadly snake.

3. GARY PLAYER

Gary Player and Jack Nicklaus were matched in an exhibition in Zwartkop, South Africa, in 1966. The round was disrupted when the golfing greats were attacked by a swarm of killer bees. Player and Nicklaus escaped unstung and wisely agreed to halve the hole rather than replay it.

4. JACK NEWTON

Jack Newton is best remembered for finishing second to Tom Watson at the 1975 British Open. Newton led the Cock o' the North Tournament in Ndola, Zambia, when he came to the 17th hole. His shot landed next to a nest of African ants. Newton was attacked by the ferocious ants, which ran up his leg. Bitten repeatedly, Newton tore off his clothes and ran off the course. The next day, Newton noticed an attractive spectator suffering the same fate. She began to run while removing her clothes. Despite the ant attack, Newton won the tournament.

5. JOHN MORGAN

John Morgan was attacked by a rat at the 1968 British Open, played at Carnoustie in Scotland. On the 10th fairway, a rat, which had run out from the bushes, bit Morgan. The bite was not serious, and Morgan was able to finish his round.

6. SUSAN ROWLANDS

Susan Rowlands displayed remarkable concentration during the 1978 Welsh Girls Tournament in Abergale. Just as she was about to putt, a mouse ran up her leg. Undeterred, Rowlands calmly sank the putt and won the tournament.

7. SAM SNEAD

On a goodwill tour of South America, Sam Snead met a birdie he did not like. He was preparing to hit a bunker shot when he was attacked by an ostrich. The big bird was a pet that had wandered onto the course. The ostrich was interested in Snead's trademark straw hat. When Snead put up his hand to protect his face, the ostrich bit him on the hand, and Snead was unable to play golf for two weeks.

8. ST. ANDREWS TROPHY

The 1984 St. Andrews Trophy, played at the Staunton Golf Course in England, nearly ended in tragedy. On the 18th hole, a herd of 50 cows, which had wandered onto the course, began a stampede. Several golfers were in the path of the runaway herd. At the last minute, the stampede was halted by the yells of players and officials.

9. MOLLY WHITAKER

Molly Whitaker literally had a monkey on her back while playing a round at the Beachwood Golf Course in Natal, South Africa. She was about to hit a shot from a sand trap when a monkey leaped from a tree and grabbed her around the neck. Luckily, her caddie chased the monkey away.

10. TOMMY ARMOUR

Tommy Armour was a champion golfer and is widely considered as the greatest golf instructor of all time. However, Armour did have an unsettling habit. During golf lessons, he liked to shoot at chipmunks with a .22-caliber rifle. The less talented the pupil, the more Armour practiced his shooting. One unhappy student asked, "When are you going to stop that and take care of me?" Armour gave him a chilling look and replied, "Don't tempt me."

Unsafe at Any Distance

Playing with these golfers can be hazardous to your health.

1. SPIRO AGNEW

Spiro Agnew, the controversial vice president to Richard Nixon, was a terror on the links. His misguided shots struck many spectators during his pro-am appearances. In 1970, he hooked a 3-wood shot that hit professional golfer Doug Sanders in the head. Sanders finished the round with his head wrapped in a bandage. Agnew's low point as a golfer came at the 1971 Bob Hope Desert Classic, in Palm Springs, California. After striking three spectators with his first two shots, Agnew retired for the day in the interest of public safety. Agnew gave golf balls to spectators hit by his shots, that read, "You have just been hit by Spiro Agnew." Bob Hope joked that when Agnew yelled "Fore!" that he was not sure if he was warning spectators or if he was counting the number of people hit by one of his shots.

2. **GERALD FORD**

Bob Hope joked, "Gerald Ford is a hit man for the PGA." The former president competed in numerous pro-ams, much to the chagrin of his galleries. At the 1995 Bob Hope Chrysler Classic, Ford struck a 71-year-old woman in the nose with a wayward shot. The woman required 10 stitches to close the wound. Bob Hope said that Ford did not need to keep score; he just counted the wounded.

3. **MARGARET MCNEIL**

Margaret McNeil and Earlena Adams played in the finals of the 1980 Boone Golf Club Championship, in North Carolina. The players were preparing for a playoff when McNeil accidentally struck Adams on her backswing, breaking her arm. With her opponent unable to continue, McNeil was declared the winner.

4. **JOHN F. KENNEDY**

John F. Kennedy often played golf with his close friend George Smathers, a senator from Florida. Although Kennedy was a terrible golf cart driver, he insisted on driving when he played. During a round at the Palm Beach Country Club in Florida, Kennedy tried to cross a narrow pedestrian bridge. The golf cart flipped over, briefly pinning Smathers beneath the water. The two drenched golfers climbed out of the water and continued their round.

5. **BUD HOELSCHER**

Bud Hoelscher hit two men with one shot at the 1952 Los Angeles Open. His approach shot struck a cameraman on the hand. The ball then hit an announcer in the face and bounced onto the green. Hoelscher two-putted from 40 feet for par.

6. DICK CRANDALL

In 1978, golfer Fred Farris was hit by a golf ball on the 16th hole of the Highland Meadows Golf Club in Sylvania, Ohio— twice in one week. Incredibly, both shots were hit by the same golfer, Dick Crandall.

7. GEORGE BUSH

Former president George Bush was a participant at the 1993 Doug Sanders Celebrity Classic in Kingwood, Texas. One of his drives struck Dan Quayle, his vice president, on top of his head. Fortunately, Quayle was not injured.

8. MAC MCLENDON

Mac McLendon hit an errant tee shot on the first hole of the second round of the 1979 Masters. The shot struck McLendon's wife, Joan, on the collarbone. She was not seriously injured, but the shaken McLendon missed the cut.

9. WILLIE DUNN

Willie Dunn used an experimental ball during an exhibition match at St. Andrews, New York. The pneumatic ball was a rubber-coated ball filled with compressed air. Dunn sliced a shot into the gallery, where it exploded, injuring several spectators.

10. **BARRY GOLDWATER**

Barry Goldwater was a senator from Arizona and the 1964 Republican candidate for president. Goldwater and professional partner Sam Snead teamed in the Phoenix Open Pro-Am. One of Goldwater's shots hit a spectator standing 30 yards away. Goldwater explained, "That guy was standing too close to my ball." The team of Snead and Goldwater won the Pro-Am.

Quicksand Traps

Golf is occasionally a dangerous game. The perils can come from the most unexpected sources. In 1969, Peggy Wilson was leading a local tournament in Miami, Florida, when she was struck in the eye by her own tee. Suffering from blurred vision, she dropped out of contention. During the filming of the golf movie *The Legend of Bagger Vance,* actor Matt Damon separated his rib cage while taking a swing.

1. BAYLY MACARTHUR

In 1931, Bayly MacArthur nearly lost his life at a tournament in New South Wales, Australia. MacArthur hit a shot into a sand trap. Only after he had stepped into the bunker did he realize that the sand was quicksand. Other golfers pulled MacArthur to safety in the nick of time.

2. TOM WEISKOPF

Tom Weiskopf nearly died in a freak accident at the Loch Lomond Golf Course, which he designed. The champion golfer became a course designer once his playing days on the PGA Tour were over. In 1990, Weiskopf was in Scotland overseeing the construction of the course. In the middle of the night, he walked onto the course to get an idea of where to locate the 14th green. He fell into a peat bog and began sinking into the muck. With no one there to help him, it appeared that he might die. Fortunately, he was able to grab a tree root and gradually pull himself free. The bog had sucked off all his clothes except the shirt on his back.

3. AL CAPONE

Al "Scarface" Capone was the most famous gangster in America, but on the golf course he was his own worst enemy. Capone always carried a gun in his golf bag for protection. During a round in 1928 at the Burnham Woods Golf Course near Chicago, the gun went off accidentally, shooting Scarface in the foot.

4. BOB RUSSELL

Bob Russell got the shock of his life while playing golf at a municipal golf course in Ohio in 1974. When he hit one of his golf balls, he discovered that he was shot. The impact of his swing had set off a bullet that was lodged in the ground. Luckily, it merely grazed his leg.

5. BOBBY CRUICKSHANK

Bobby Cruickshank led the 1934 U.S. Open Championship, played at the Merion Golf Course in Pennsylvania, when he hit a shot headed for a water hazard on the 11th hole. Miraculously, the ball skipped across the water and landed on the green. Cruickshank threw his club in the air in celebration. His joy ended as the airborne club came down and struck him on the head, rendering him unconscious.

Cruickshank stumbled through the final holes in a daze. He shot 76 and finished in third place.

6. **GARY PLAYER**

Gary Player came to the final hole of the 1955 Egyptian Matchplay Championship needing a 5 to win. His drive came to rest next to a wall. Player's next shot ricocheted off the wall and hit him, knocking him out cold. Player recovered and somehow managed to shoot a 4 on the hole for an apparent victory. However, at that point, he received the bad news that he had been assessed a two-stroke penalty for being struck by the ball.

7. **JIM ARMSTRONG**

In 1963, Jim Armstrong played a round at the Desert Forest Golf Club in Carefree, Arizona, that was anything but carefree. On the second hole, Armstrong's drive bounced off a tee marker and struck him on the head. After regaining his senses, he tried again. This time the drive ricocheted off the same marker and hit him in the knee. Not willing to risk further injury, he wisely picked up his ball and skipped the hole.

8. **RICHARD BOXALL**

Richard Boxall got a bad break at the 1991 British Open, played at Royal Birkdale. He was only three shots off the lead when he felt a sharp pain in his leg while swinging a club. He had broken his leg during the swing and was forced to withdraw.

9. **TONY LEMA**

Tony Lema narrowly avoided serious injury at the 1957 Bing Crosby National Pro-Am, at Pebble Beach, California. On the difficult ninth hole, Lema hit a good shot and jumped for joy. Standing too near one of the cliffs that overlook the bay, he tumbled down a steep embankment. Lema survived the fall, but suffered bumps and bruises.

10. **ROCCO MEDIATE**

Rocco Mediate was on a roll when he won the 2000 Buick Open. The next week he was relaxing outside the clubhouse before the first round when his chair collapsed. Mediate injured his neck, shoulder, and lower back. His first round of 77 put him out of contention.

Overcoming Handicaps

These golfers proved that no handicap is too great to overcome.

1. JIM TAYLOR

Jim Taylor lost both his arms in a childhood accident. Amazingly, he overcame his handicap to become an outstanding golfer. Using his artificial arms, Taylor made eight holes-in-one at the Golf Green Golf Center in Longview, Washington.

2. MARGARET WALDRON

Margaret Waldron made her first hole-in-one on March 18, 1990, on the seventh hole at the Long Point Golf Course on Amelia Island, Florida. What made this feat so remarkable was that Waldron was 74 years old and legally blind. Her husband, Pete, advised her of the direction and distance of shots, thus enabling her to play the game. Incredibly, she aced the same hole the next day.

3. CY YOUNG

Cy Young lost his left arm in a childhood accident. On January 28, 1995, at the Lakeview Golf Course in Delray Beach, Florida, the 70-year-old golfer made two holes-in-one in the same round. Young aced both the first and 13th holes.

4. JIMMY NICHOLS

Jimmy Nichols was a one-armed golfer who, in 1933, hit a shot that would make Tiger Woods envious. Nichols aced a par-4 336-yard hole on a golf course in Douglas, Georgia.

5. THOMAS M'AULIFFE

Thomas M'Auliffe was an armless golfer who played by holding the club between his right shoulder and cheek. Using this unorthodox style, he once shot a round of 108 at the Buffalo Country Links in New York.

6. FRANK KAARTO

Frank Kaarto, a 70-year-old golfer, hit a hole-in-one on the third hole of the Wyandotte Hills Golf Course in Twin Lakes, Michigan, on August 29, 1985. Kaarto aced the hole despite having no left arm and blurred vision in his right eye.

7. CHARLES BOSWELL

Charles Boswell played for Alabama in the 1937 Rose Bowl. In 1944, Boswell was attempting to rescue a friend in a battle in Germany when he was blinded by an exploding shell. Boswell took up golf in 1946. He was a 17-time winner of the United States Blind Golfers Association and made a hole-in-one in 1970. For many years, Boswell hosted his own celebrity tournament in Birmingham, Alabama. His best round was an 81.

8. **TOMMY ARMOUR**

Tommy Armour was severely wounded during World War I. A mustard gas attack blinded him in the left eye. As a member of the British Tank Corps, he suffered eight shrapnel wounds in his shoulder and needed a metal plate inserted in his head. Despite the injuries, between 1927 and 1931, Armour won the U.S. Open Championship, PGA Championship, and British Open.

9. **ED FURGOL**

At the age of 12, Ed Furgol shattered his left elbow in a playground accident. The accident left Furgol with a crooked, withered arm. He overcame the odds by winning the 1954 U.S. Open Championship and was named PGA Player of the Year.

10. **J. W. PERRET**

It is said that you cannot kill two birds with one stone. Golfer J. W. Perret proved that you can kill two gulls with two tee shots. Perret was a competitor in the 1935 Society of One Armed Golfers Championship at Troon, Scotland. His tee shots on the first two holes struck and killed sea gulls.

In Sickness and in Health

These golfers overcame illness and injury.

1. BABE ZAHARIAS

In 1953, Babe Zaharias, one of the best golfers on the women's tour, was diagnosed with cancer. It appeared that her golf career was over. Zaharias refused to quit and capped her amazing comeback with a 12-shot victory in the 1954 U.S. Women's Open Championship, at the Salem Country Club in Peabody, Massachusetts.

2. BEN HOGAN

Ben Hogan was one of the best golfers on the PGA Tour when he was involved in a near-fatal automobile accident in Texas on February 2, 1949. The car he was driving was hit head-on by a Greyhound bus. Just before impact, Hogan threw himself across his wife on the passenger seat, a move that saved both their lives; the steering wheel was driven through the back of the driver's seat. Hogan suffered a broken collarbone, fractured ribs, two pelvic fractures, and two

Babe Didrikson Zaharias

Babe Didrikson Zaharias enjoyed one of the most successful athletic careers in women's sports history, successively succeeding at basketball, track and field, and golf. She succumbed to cancer in 1956 at the age of 42.

cracked bones in his left ankle. Not only did Hogan return to the tour, but he played his greatest golf after the accident. Hogan won the U.S. Open Championship only a year after the accident and in 1953 won all three major tournaments he entered.

3. GENE LITTLER

Gene Littler was diagnosed with cancer of the lymph glands in 1972. Littler recovered from the dreaded illness and won a tournament in 1973 and had one of his best years in 1975, when he won three times at age 45.

4. SHELLEY HAMLIN

In one of golf's most inspirational stories, Shelley Hamlin won the 1992 Phar-Mor at Inverrary Tournament on the LPGA Tour. Only seven months earlier, she had undergone a mastectomy for breast cancer. The victory was Hamlin's first since 1978.

5. PAUL AZINGER

Paul Azinger was at the peak of his career when he was diagnosed with cancer soon after winning the 1993 PGA Championship. He missed the 1994 PGA Tour season, and his career was in jeopardy. Azinger's comeback was complete when he won the 2000 Sony Open in Hawaii.

6. KIM WILLIAMS

Kim Williams was only two shots off the lead at the 1994 Youngstown-Warren Classic, an LPGA tournament played in Ohio. Following the round, she was wounded by a stray bullet shot by a man taking target practice a mile away. Despite having a bullet lodged in her ribs, Williams competed in the

Jamie Farr Toledo Classic the following week. She finished tenth, her best showing of the year.

7. SCOTT VERPLANK

Scott Verplank displayed great promise by winning the 1985 Western Open while still an amateur. His career declined as he was beset by injury and illness. Three elbow surgeries hampered Verplank's swing, and he had to wear an insulin pump to control his diabetes. At his nadir, Verplank missed 24 cuts in a row in 1991. Verplank overcame these obstacles and won the 2000 Reno-Tahoe Open, his first victory on the PGA Tour in twelve years.

8. TOM SHAW

Tom Shaw suffered a broken back in a 1966 automobile accident. He won four PGA tournaments following the accident, including the 1971 Bing Crosby Pro-Am.

9. CASEY MARTIN

Casey Martin was one of Tiger Woods's teammates on the Stanford golf team. The talented golfer's career was jeopardized by a circulatory ailment in his right leg that made it painful for him to walk. Since the PGA Tour did not permit players to use golf carts, Martin's dream to be a professional golfer appeared to be over. However, Martin won a court case that allowed him to use a cart, and in 2000, he played on the PGA Tour.

10. STEVE ELKINGTON

Steve Elkington won the prestigious Players Championship in 1991. The Australian experienced a slump in 1994, and upon medical examination it was discovered that he had developed an allergy to grass, a serious obstacle for a professional golfer. Elkington had to take two shots a day and a dozen pills to combat the allergy. In 1995, he won the PGA Championship, his first major.

Death in the Afternoon

These golfers died either while playing or in their prime.

1. HAROLD KALLES

In 1963, at a golf course in Toronto, Canada, Harold Kalles was hitting a bunker shot when he hit a tree on his follow-through. The shaft broke and the sharp edge pierced his throat, killing him.

2. DAVID BARNET

In 1914, David Barnet, a soldier in the English army, was training on the field next to the Wormit Golf Course in Fifeshire, England. At the same time, a women's tournament was being held. An errant shot struck Barnet in the temple, and he died two days later.

3. ANTHONY HUNT

In August 2000, Anthony Hunt, a golfer at the Marlborough Country Club in Massachusetts, was run over and killed by a golf cart. The runaway cart was driven by an 85-year-old golfer who had accidentally stepped on the accelerator instead of the brake.

4. PAYNE STEWART

In one of golf's greatest tragedies, Payne Stewart, the reigning United States Open champion, was killed in a plane crash on October 25, 1999. The 42-year-old winner of three major championships was on a private jet that crashed in South Dakota.

5. TONY LEMA

"Champagne" Tony Lema, the 1964 British Open champion, died in a plane crash on July 24, 1966. Lema was flying from the PGA Championship to an exhibition in Chicago when his private plane crashed on a golf course, the Sportsmen's Club, in Lansing, Illinois. The plane came to rest in a water hazard on the seventh hole.

6. WILLIE ANDERSON

Between 1901 and 1905, Willie Anderson won the U.S. Open Championship four times. In 1910, the Scotsman died of arteriosclerosis, at the age of 31.

7. TOM MORRIS, JR.

In 1868, Tom Morris, Jr. won his first British Open, at the age of 18. It was the first of four consecutive British Open championships for Morris. He died in 1875, at the age of 25, shortly after the death of his wife.

8. MARVIN WORSHAM

Marvin Worsham, younger brother of well-known golfer Lew Worsham, died in an automobile accident in North Carolina on October 22, 1950. The 20-year-old Wake Forest student was a promising player. Arnold Palmer, his teammate on the Wake Forest golf team and close friend, was so shaken by his death that he briefly gave up golf.

9. TED MAKALENA

Ted Makalena won the 1966 Hawaiian Open. The 34-year-old golfer died on September 13, 1968, five days after breaking his neck by diving into shallow water on Waikiki Beach.

10. FREDDIE TAIT

Freddie Tait was one of the most charismatic golfers at the turn of the twentieth century. The popular golfer was shot and killed while fighting for Great Britain in the Boer War in South Africa in February 1900.

The 18th Hole

H ere are some notable golf lasts.

1. JOHNNY GOODMAN

The last amateur golfer to win the U.S. Open Championship was Johnny Goodman, who finished first in the 1933 U.S. Open, played at the North Shore Country Club in Glenview, Illinois. Goodman was the fifth and final amateur to win the Open.

2. PHIL MICKELSON

The last amateur to win a tournament on the PGA Tour was Phil Mickelson. He won the 1991 Northern Telecom Tucson Open. Mickelson lived up to his early promise by becoming one of the dominant players of the 1990s.

3. LIONEL HEBERT

The last PGA Championship to be conducted in match play format was the 1957 tournament, played at the Miami Valley

Country Club in Dayton, Ohio. Lionel Hebert defeated Dow
Finsterwald 2 and 1 in the championship match. The next
year the tournament was converted to stroke play.

4. SANDRA PALMER

Sandra Palmer won the 1972 Titleholders Championship, at
the Pine Needles Golf and Country Club in Southern Pines,
North Carolina. The tournament was one of the four major
tournaments on the LPGA Tour. Due to financial problems,
the tournament was discontinued after the 1972 event.

5. SAM SNEAD

Sam Snead was 52 years old when he won the 1965 Greater
Greensboro Open, making him the oldest player ever to win
on the PGA Tour. It was the eighth time Snead had won the
event and the last of his record 81 victories.

6. JACK NICKLAUS

Jack Nicklaus finished his career on the PGA Tour in style.
The 46-year-old Golden Bear shot 30 on the back nine of
the final round to win the 1986 Masters. It was his eighteenth and final major championship and his last victory on
the PGA Tour.

7. ARNOLD PALMER

The last player to lead the PGA Tour in prize money and
earn less than $100,000 in a year was Arnold Palmer. He
topped all golfers with $81,448 in 1962. The next season
Palmer led the money list with earnings of $128,230.

8. HUGH KIRKALDY

Hugh Kirkaldy won the 1891 British Open, played at St. Andrews, with a 36-hole total of 166. It was the last British Open played in a 36-hole format. The following year, the tournament was expanded to its present 72-hole format.

9. TOMMY ARMOUR

Tommy Armour was the last golfer to win the U.S. Open Championship with a 72-hole score of more than 300. Armour won the 1927 Open, played at the Oakmont Country Club, with a winning score of 301.

10. BOBBY JONES

The last golfer to win the U.S. Open and U.S. Amateur Championships in the same year was Bobby Jones. Jones accomplished the double in 1930, the year he won the Grand Slam.

Fantastic Finishes

L et us go out on a winning note with some of golf's most fantastic finishes.

1. JERRY BARBER

Forty-five-year-old Jerry Barber finished with a flourish to win the 1961 PGA Championship, played at the Olympic Fields Country Club in Illinois. Barber sank putts of 20, 40, and 60 feet on the last three holes to tie Don January. Barber shot a 67 to win the playoff by one stroke.

2. LEW WORSHAM

Lew Worsham holed a 135-yard iron shot on the final hole to win the 1953 World Championship in Chicago. The dramatic shot was the highlight of the first nationally televised golf tournament.

3. PATTY BERG

Patty Berg made a 35-foot eagle putt on the final hole to win her sixth Women's Western Open by one shot over Wiffi Smith. The Western Open was considered a major tournament on the LPGA Tour at the time.

4. HALE IRWIN

Hale Irwin sank a 45-foot putt on the final hole of the 1990 U.S. Open Championship, played at the Medinah Country Club in Illinois. The 45-year-old Irwin defeated Mike Donald in a playoff, to win his third U.S. Open title.

5. PAUL LAWRIE

Paul Lawrie began the final round of the 1999 British Open 10 shots behind leader Jean Van de Velde. The Scotsman won the tournament in a playoff, completing the greatest one-day comeback in British Open history.

6. GEORGE DUNCAN

George Duncan trailed leader Abe Mitchell by 13 shots at the midpoint of the 1920 British Open, played at the Deal Golf Course in England. Duncan charged to a two-stroke victory.

7. JACKIE BURKE

Jackie Burke seemed out of contention when he began the final round of the 1956 Masters eight shots behind the leader, amateur Ken Venturi. The 24-year-old Venturi bogeyed six of the last nine holes. Burke took advantage of Venturi's collapse to win his first Masters.

8. ARNOLD PALMER

Arnold Palmer's greatest charge came at the 1960 U.S. Open Championship, played at the Cherry Hills Country Club outside Denver, Colorado. Palmer trailed leader Mike Souchak by seven strokes with 18 holes to play, but a final round of 65 gave Palmer the victory.

9. **PAYNE STEWART**

Payne Stewart shot a 31 on the back nine to win the 1989 PGA Championship, played at the Kemper Lakes Golf Course in Illinois. Stewart birdied four of the last five holes on his way to victory.

10. **TIGER WOODS**

Tiger Woods finished with a flourish to win the 2000 PGA Grand Slam of Golf, played at Poipu Beach, Hawaii. He eagled the final hole, forcing a playoff with Vijay Singh. On the first playoff hole, Woods carded his second consecutive eagle to win the $400,000 first prize.

Bibliography

Alliss, Peter. *The Who's Who of Golf.* Englewood Cliffs, N.J.: Prentice Hall, 1983.

Aretha, David. *Golf Almanac.* Lincolnwood, Ill.: Publications International, 1993.

Barkow, Al. *20th Century Golf Chronicle.* Lincolnwood, Ill.: Publications International, 1993.

Campbell, Shepherd, and Peter Landau. *Presidential Lies.* New York: Macmillan, 1996.

Conner, Floyd. *Fore!* San Francisco: Chronicle Books, 1995.

———. *Golf!* San Francisco: Chronicle Books, 1992.

Dobereiner, Peter. *The Book of Golf Disasters.* New York: Atheneum, 1984.

Elliot, Len, and Barbara Kelly. *Who's Who in Golf.* New Rochelle, N.Y.: Arlington House, 1976.

Fischler, Stan, and Shirley Fischler. *The Best, Worst, and Most Unusual in Sports.* New York: Fawcett Crest, 1977.

Hope, Bob. *Confessions of a Hooker.* New York: Doubleday, 1985.

Nash, Bruce, and Allan Zullo. *Amazing True Golf Facts.* Kansas City: Andrews and McMeel, 1992.

———. *The Golf Hall of Shame.* New York: Pocket Books, 1989.

———. *The Golf Nut's Amazing Feats & Records.* Chicago: Contemporary Books, 1994.

Peper, George. *Golf in America.* New York: Harry N. Abrams, 1988.

Phillips, Louis, and Burnham Holmes. *The Complete Book of Sports Nicknames.* Los Angeles: Renaissance Books, 1994.

Sinette, Calvin. *Forbidden Fairways.* Chelsea: Sleeping Bear Press, 1998.

Sommers, Robert. *Golf Anecdotes.* New York: Oxford University Press, 1995.

Strege, John. *Tiger.* New York: Broadway Books, 1997.

Wallechinsky, David. *The Complete Book of the Olympics.* New York: Penguin, 1988.

Index

About the Author

Floyd Conner is a lifelong fan of golf and the author of eleven books. His sports books include *Baseball's Most Wanted, Football's Most Wanted, Day By Day in Cincinnati Bengals History,* and *This Date in Sports History.* He also co-authored *Day By Day in Cincinnati Reds History* and the best-selling *365 Sports Facts a Year Calendar.* He lives in Cincinnati with his wife, Susan, and son, Travis.